Scarecrow Studies in Young Adult Literature
Series Editor: Patty Campbell

Scarecrow Studies in Young Adult Literature is intended to continue the body of critical writing established in Twayne's Young Adult Authors Series and to expand it beyond single-author studies to explorations of genres, multicultural writing, and controversial issues in young adult (YA) reading. Many of the contributing authors of the series are among the leading scholars and critics of adolescent literature, and some are YA novelists themselves.

   The series is shaped by its editor, Patty Campbell, who is a renowned authority in the field, with a thirty-year background as critic, lecturer, librarian, and teacher of YA literature. Patty Campbell was the 2001 winner of the ALAN Award, given by the Assembly on Adolescent Literature of the National Council of Teachers of English for distinguished contribution to YA literature. In 1989 she was the winner of the American Library Association's Grolier Award for distinguished service to young adults and reading.

Angela Johnson

Poetic Prose

KaaVonia Hinton

*Scarecrow Studies in Young Adult
Literature, No. 23*

THE SCARECROW PRESS, INC.
Lanham, Maryland • Toronto • Oxford
2006

SCARECROW PRESS, INC.

Published in the United States of America
by Scarecrow Press, Inc.
A wholly owned subsidiary of
The Rowman & Littlefield Publishing Group, Inc.
4501 Forbes Boulevard, Suite 200, Lanham, Maryland 20706
www.scarecrowpress.com

PO Box 317
Oxford
OX2 9RU, UK

British Library Cataloguing in Publication Information Available

Library of Congress Cataloging-in-Publication Data

Hinton, KaaVonia, 1973–
  Angela Johnson : poetic prose / KaaVonia Hinton.
    p. cm. — (Scarecrow studies in young adult literature ; no. 23)
  Includes bibliographical references and index.
  ISBN-13: 978-0-8108-5092-7 (hardcover : alk. paper)
  ISBN-10: 0-8108-5092-3 (hardcover : alk. paper)
  1. Johnson, Angela, 1961– 2. Authors, American—20th century—
Biography. 3. African American authors—Biography. I. Title. II. Series.

PS3560.O37129Z55 2006
813'.54—dc22   2006001893

To Za'id, my future favorite author

With thanks to my mother for believing in me; to Patty Campbell for entrusting such an important project to me; to Angela Johnson for her wonderful talent and her willingness to share her wisdom with me; and to Richard Jackson for his contribution.

Contents

Preface

While working on a doctoral degree in English education, I took a course on young adult literature. It was summer. The course was short, and the reading list was long. As is my custom, I searched the list for familiar names and titles, particularly ones by and about blacks. When I came across Angela Johnson's name, I stopped. That's odd, I mused. She writes picture books, not young adult literature. To my surprise, Johnson had two young adult novels to her credit at the time. A quick trip to the campus bookstore confirmed that this was in fact the same Angela Johnson who had written a number of the picture books I read to my son each night. With a quick glance at the cover art, I knew the artist had to be Synthia Saint James. But what about the writer? It was clear that Johnson had talent. Her picture books were concise, poetic, and memorable. The characters were young and the themes were familiar in a way that captivated my son's attention. I wondered, Could she write compelling young adult novels? I stared at the thin book. *Toning the Sweep*, I said aloud. What is that? I had to find out. Upon opening the book and reading a few pages, I noticed that the sparse, poetic language of her picture books had made its way into her young adult novel.

I developed an immediate connection with the protagonist Emily, her mother, and her grandmother. Throughout the course of the novel, Emily gains an understanding of who she is and what she is capable of enduring. One of the ways Emily discovers her sense of self is by learning more about her grandmother, her deceased grandfather, and her mother. Right away Emily takes on this task, believing that she must accomplish it alone. She says, "Haven't really done much by myself. . . . I should find out everything about Ola on my own."[1] Videography is the vehicle Emily uses to learn about her family and, by extension, herself. While standing behind the video camera, Emily learns several shocking truths about her family history, including the source of her mother's bitterness toward Ola, her nonconventional grandmother.

During class discussions about the book, I spoke of how the novel touched me, resonating with some of my own life experiences. I was particularly taken with the passages devoted to hair, a significant part of African American expressive culture that has both astounded and puzzled me as I have struggled with the politics behind my own black hair.

After taking the course, I searched for information about Johnson. Finding very little, I grew disappointed, but I never stopped searching for more, more biographical information and more books by her. When I decided that two novels by Johnson would be a part of my dissertation, I learned that at least two other Ph.D. students before me had included her earlier novels in their studies. As my dissertation was a literary analysis of six novels by three different African American young adult authors, I chose not to interview the authors. When my dissertation was near completion, however, I had the opportunity to meet Johnson.

She came to a popular children's bookstore in Columbus, Ohio, to promote her award-winning novel *The First Part Last*. Her parents had driven her to Columbus from Kent, Ohio, as she does not have a driver's license. She talked briefly about her parents and their significance to her before moving on to talk about her books. The audience was small, which was a relief to me as I had a number of questions I had to ask about Shoogy from *Heaven*, some of the issues in her work that I considered to be black feminist, the setting of her work, and her writing process. She graciously answered my questions, but she seemed extremely quiet, introverted even. She later told us that she does not like to speak publicly. "I am probably the only author who hates to win awards for fear of having to deliver a speech," she joked. Well, with three Coretta Scott King Book Awards, a Michael L. Printz award, and the "Genius Grant" to her credit, Angela Denise Johnson not winning awards is unthinkable.

During a telephone conversation a year later, I asked Johnson if her life had changed after winning the MacArthur grant, a $500,000 stipend awarded over a five-year period. She said, "My life hasn't changed. I think awards are wonderful things. The MacArthur grant is wonderful because it is all about what you will do in the future; the idea that they believe you have so much more to come is a wonderful thing. Getting to know the other MacArthur fellows, who are quite amazing, has enriched me. I write books for kids, and that's wonderful, but these people [the other MacArthur grant recipients] who are judging the age of the universe and conservationists and people who are affecting change worldwide are amazing, and the idea that I was thought of is amazing; but, no, it hasn't changed me, and it won't change me." She continued, "I live the same way. I didn't go on any extravagant vacation; I didn't buy an expensive car. I don't have a car. I don't drive. My life hasn't changed. And I still live in this 111-year-old Victorian house." When asked if she felt pressured to produce more quality work, she said, "The only pressure that I feel surrounds being responsible for the money, making sure that it is not wasted, making sure it educates my nieces and nephews and funds the organizations that are really close to my heart. My responsibility is to keep doing what I'm doing, to keep writing."

A few months after our telephone conversation, our second meeting occurred when she invited me to her home in Kent, Ohio, shortly after her busy summer filled with travel, including a trip to the American Library Association conference to deliver an acceptance speech for the Michael L. Printz and Coretta Scott King author awards, both for *The First Part Last*. I made the trip to Kent from Okemos, Michigan, by car. As I drove closer to Kent, I began to recognize names of places connected to Johnson. There was Cleveland, Ohio, the city she lived in when Richard Jackson called to tell her that *Tell Me a Story, Mama* would be published. So much of Johnson's experience in Cleveland, wandering down streets and in and out of museums, coffee shops, and diners, appears in her books set in urban centers, such as *Humming Whispers*. Seeing the sign for Ravenna, Ohio, brought to mind Johnson's work there as a child-development worker with Volunteers in Service to America. Windham, Ohio, is the town where Johnson grew up, and of course the final sign "Welcome to Kent, Ohio," signals the place where Johnson had the courage to end her pursuit of a teaching career in an effort to become a writer. In Kent, Johnson was surrounded by people connected to youth literature: Cynthia Rylant, Dav Pilkey, and Rhonda Mitchell, to name a few who crossed her path.

It was hot the morning Johnson greeted me on her porch and welcomed me into the two-story house once occupied by Captain Underpants. She was dressed comfortably in a tan oversized sweatshirt and black sweatpants. As I followed her into her den, we talked about gardening, particularly the mint garden she had planted alongside her garage. While we chatted, I enjoyed the distant smell of mint as I eyed her bookshelf, noting familiar and also recently published titles such as Bill Clinton's *My Life*. Johnson offered to get me a drink and some fruit before comfortably sitting on the sofa and laughing when the conversation turned to Captain Underpants. She told me to tell my six-year-old son, a diehard Captain Underpants fan, that her niece Ashley now occupies his office. Johnson is sincere, modest, and incredibly funny. She is what some might call "down to earth." During the two-hour interview, the voices of teenage girls appropriately lingered in the background as Johnson's niece and her friends enjoyed the beautiful summer day. Gardening, the Civil Rights Movement, shopping, and listening to Mos Def was just as much a part of our conversations as critics, young adult audiences, and the African American literary tradition. The interview was informal, closer to a dialogue between acquaintances. She generously shared her passions, beliefs, and opinions with me, not only about the creation of her work, but also about its purpose. My conversations with Johnson in her home, via e-mail, and on the telephone are the source of undocumented quotations by her unless otherwise indicated. This volume focuses on Johnson's life and looks critically at her work, which spans several genres, including poetry, novels, and short stories.

Since the publication of *Toning the Sweep*, Johnson has written eleven other young adult books, including short stories and two books of poetry. She has also contributed short stories to a number of noteworthy young adult collections, such as *Memories of Sun: Stories of Africa and America*, edited by Jane Kurtz; *The Color of Absence: 12 Stories about Loss and Hope*, edited by James Howe; *Love and Sex: Ten Stories of Truth*, edited by Michael Cart; and *One Hot Second: Stories about Desire*, edited by Cathy Young. Presently, she is working on a third book featuring characters in *Heaven*. With over forty books to her credit, including board books, middle-grade novels and young adult literature, Johnson, who refers to her writing as unschooled and undisciplined, has made a major contribution to the field.

NOTE

1. Angela Johnson, *Toning the Sweep*. (New York: Orchard, 1993), 22 (hereafter cited as *Toning*).

Chronology

1961 Angela Denise Johnson born June 18, Tuskegee, Alabama, the first child of Arthur and Truzetta Johnson.

1962 Johnson family moves to Diamond, Ohio.

1966 Johnson family, including baby brothers Warren Keith and Jeffrey Kent, move to Windham, Ohio.

1969 Johnson begins keeping a journal.

1979 Johnson visits Spain. Graduates from Windham High School. Enters Kent State University and majors in special education.

1981–1982 Johnson works with Volunteers in Service to America (VISTA) as a child-development worker.

1982 Johnson chooses not to register for classes. Becomes a nanny and commits to honing her craft as a writer.

1983 Johnson begins babysitting for Cynthia Rylant. Reads Virginia Hamilton's *Sweet Whispers, Brother Rush*.

1986 Cynthia Rylant encourages Johnson to send three picture-book manuscripts—*Tell Me a Story, Mama*; *Julius*; and *Down the Winding Road*—to Richard Jackson at Orchard Books.

1989   Johnson becomes a freelance writer and publishes *Tell Me a Story, Mama*, which wins a Best Books citation, *School Library Journal*.

1990   Johnson publishes *Do Like Kyla* and *When I Am Old with You*, which is recognized as a Notable Social Studies Trade Book for Young People by the National Council for the Social Studies.

1991   *When I Am Old with You* named Coretta Scott King Honor Book and earns the American Library Association Social Responsibilities Round Table Award and the Ezra Jack Keats New Writer Award. Johnson receives the Northern Ohio Live Writers Award. Cynthia Rylant leaves a copy of Francesca Lia Block's *Weetzie Bat* on Johnson's porch.

1992   Johnson publishes *One of Three*.

1993   Johnson publishes *The Girl Who Wore Snakes*, *Julius*, *The Leaving Morning*, and *Toning the Sweep*. American Library Association Best Books for Young Adults citation, *School Library Journal*, for *Toning the Sweep*. Johnson receives the Alabama Author Award.

1994   Johnson wins the Coretta Scott King Book Award and Booklist Editors' Choice for *Toning the Sweep*. Publishes *Joshua by the Sea*, *Joshua's Night Whispers*, *Mama Bird, Baby Birds*, and *Rain Feet*.

1995   Johnson wins PEN/Norma Klein Award for Children's Fiction. Publishes *Humming Whispers* and *Shoes Like Miss Alice's*. *Humming Whispers* noted as an ALA Quick Pick selection.

1996   Johnson publishes *The Aunt in Our House* and "Flying Away" in *But That's Another Story: Famous Authors Introduce Popular Genres*.

1997   Johnson publishes *Daddy Calls Me Man* and *The Rolling Store*; "Family is What You Have" in *Horn Book*; "Tuesday (Chattanooga, TN)" in *In Praise of Our Fathers and Our Mothers: A Black Family Treasury by Outstanding Authors and Artists*; "Her Daddy's Hands" in *In Daddy's Arms I Am Tall: African Americans Celebrating Fathers*.

1998   Johnson publishes *Gone from Home: Short Takes*; *Maniac Monkeys on Magnolia Street*; *Heaven*; *Songs of Faith*; and *The Other Side:*

Shorter Poems. Wins the Coretta Scott King Book Award and a Best Book for Young Adults citation from ALA for *Heaven*. *The Other Side: Shorter Poems* named Coretta Scott King Honor Book and the Lee Bennett Hopkins Poetry Award. *Songs of Faith* listed as an *American Bookseller* Pick of the Lists.

1999   Johnson publishes *The Wedding*. *The Other Side: Shorter Poems* is recognized as a Notable Social Studies Trade Books for Young People by the National Council for the Social Studies.

2000   Johnson publishes *Down the Winding Road*, *Those Building Men*, and *When Mules Flew on Magnolia Street*, which is chosen as one of the Black Caucus of the American Library Association's Top 20 Children's books.

2001   Johnson publishes *Running Back to Ludie*; "Watcher" in *Love & Sex: Ten Stories of Truth*; "Through a Window" in *On the Fringe*; "Atomic Blue Pieces" in *The Color of Absence: 12 Stories about Loss and Hope*.

2002   Johnson publishes *Looking for Red*; "A Kind of Music" in *One Hot Second: Stories about Desire*; "From Above" in *Heart to Heart: New Poems Inspired by Twentieth-Century American Art*. *Those Building Men* is recognized as a Notable Social Studies Trade Books for Young People by the National Council for the Social Studies.

2003   Johnson is winner of the MacArthur Fellowship. Publishes *I Dream of Trains*, *Just Like Josh Gibson*, and *The First Part Last*.

2004   Johnson wins the Coretta Scott King and Michael L. Printz Awards for *The First Part Last*, which is listed as an ALA Best Books for Young Adults, an ALA Quick Pick for Reluctant Young Adult Readers, and a Booklist Editor's Choice. *Just Like Josh Gibson* named one of *Black Issues Book Review* Best Books of 2004. Publishes *Violet's Music* and *Bird*; "A Girl Like Me" in *On Her Way: Stories and Poems about Growing Up Girl*; "Our Song" in *Memories of Sun: Stories of Africa and America*; "Tripping over the Lunch Lady" in *Tripping over the Lunch Lady: And other School Stories*.

2005   Johnson publishes *A Sweet Smell of Roses*.

Chapter One

Discovering the Inner Voice

Because we were in the middle of the country, we did all of the things that kids in the country did, like picking blackberries, staying in the woods all day, and building forts. We'd be gone all day long. Most of our parents worked. And we'd leave home, go in the woods to the creek, and catch frogs. It was the typical life of sort of a country kid. Since everyone knew everyone else, we weren't really afraid of anything.

Angela Johnson's career as an award-winning young adult novelist almost didn't happen. Like so many would-be writers, she had decided to pursue a more financially stable career, teaching. But in the end, Johnson abandoned the familiar, and seemingly more secure, and became an author.

Angela Denise Johnson was born on June 18, 1961, in Tuskegee, Alabama, to Arthur and Truzetta Hall Johnson. Johnson was the couple's first child. Two sons, Warren Keith and Jeffrey Kent, soon followed in 1964 and 1965 respectively. When Johnson was just over a year old, her father moved the family to Diamond, Ohio, to take advantage of the opportunities afforded blacks in the North. A few years later the family moved again, this time to Windham, Ohio, where Johnson's parents continue to live today, Arthur as a retired General Motors employee and Truzetta as an employee in a social services agency.

Although Johnson easily adapted to rural life in the small midwestern town where no one locked their doors at night, she maintained her connection to Alabama, returning at least once a year to visit family and friends. This connection to the South permeates much of Johnson's work, from *Toning the Sweep* to the more recent *Bird*.

Johnson describes her childhood as normal. "The wonderful part was it was so normal that when I decided I wanted to be a writer, my parents didn't tell me I couldn't. They were supportive. There were no writers in my family, but they didn't see that as a problem. It wasn't a big issue with them." Johnson first made the decision to become a writer in third grade. She once commented, "I knew that I wanted to be a writer when my third-grade teacher read me and my class *Harriet the Spy*. I wanted to tell stories like that."[1] Impressed most often by the stories Ms. Wilma Mitchell read to the third graders about "powerful girls," girls Johnson chooses to make the center of much of her own fiction, Johnson says, "Ms. Mitchell was very influential. It was during the time when teachers still had the time to read to kids after recess. She would lower the lights. We would put our heads down, and she would read to us. The only punishment she could give us was no reading. It was devastating."

Johnson recorded her thoughts in diaries and later began writing what she calls "punk poetry." When discussing teen angst, Johnson says, "I sort of poured mine out in writing bad punk poetry—really angry poetry that they wouldn't put in the literary journal. So I'm not in any of the old literary journals at my high school. My poetry was too angry for them. They said 'You're always talking about inner-city buildings collapsing and miserable stuff.'" Though inner-city buildings are not necessarily collapsing in Johnson's recent writing, her topics continue to be serious and sometimes bleak. The pending death of a beloved grandmother, the demise of a mentally ill sister, the drowning of a brother, homelessness, teen pregnancy, and neglect are all issues Johnson covers in her work, issues that could be described as "miserable stuff."

Few blacks lived in Windham; probably as few as 2 percent made up the population, yet Johnson maintains that blacks were immersed in the social life of the town from its beginning. She takes pride in knowing that documentation of the existence of blacks in the town extends to the 1800s, at least. She is also quick to point out that blacks in the schools, though few in number, were quite visible in athletics, including the cheerleading squad, and in student government. Johnson was thankful for the progressive beliefs of her teachers—teachers willing to confront

racism, overt and unintentional. Johnson recalls an incident that occurred in fifth grade when a close friend offered other members of the
class an invitation to an upcoming birthday party but told Johnson her
father forbade her to invite Johnson because she was black. Johnson
says of her classmate, "She didn't have a clue that what she was telling
me was offensive or terrible." But Johnson's teacher knew. The teacher
asked the little girl to retrieve all of the invitations she had given out and
sent a note home to the child's parents. Reflecting on the incident Johnson says, "I consider myself very lucky just to have had them [progres-
sive teachers], and I think it did take a lot of the sting out of growing up
in an area where many times in my social life I was the only black face."

Partly because of teachers influenced by what Johnson calls the hip-
pie culture of the seventies, Johnson describes junior high as the best
time in her life. Her teachers were young, recent graduates from sur-
rounding schools like Kent State and Youngstown State University who
were open to new methods of teaching and interacting with youth. But
racial isolation was still an issue for Johnson. "I was a popular kid. I did
all of the things you were supposed to do, but there were times when I
would look around me, and I understood that racially and culturally I
was a bit separate. I stood there as an African American young woman,
and most of my friends weren't." Johnson describes this sense of racial
disconnect as "less about race and more about understanding," a sentiment expressed in many of her young adult novels.

She was a member of the cheerleading squad and active in school or-
ganizations as well, but during her teen years she always felt there was
more to life than what she saw around her. "I was missing something
living in a small town." She says reading biographies, travel literature,
and magazines like the *Village Voice* enlightened her, while others in her
community seemed to be a "bit limited in their scope."

Though Johnson knew writing was important to her, she admits that
when she graduated from Windham High School in 1979 her career
goals were unclear. She decided to major in special education and prepare to teach. However, her inner voice would not allow it. After three
years of studying to become a special-education teacher at Kent State
University in northeastern Ohio, Johnson got serious about becoming a
writer. Convinced that being a teacher would prevent her from writing,
she stopped registering for classes, became a nanny, and committed to
writing virtually full-time.

As a full-time writer, Johnson wrote poetry and what she calls vignettes, similar to what is found in *The Other Side: Shorter Poems* and *Running Back to Ludie*. At that time, she had never even considered writing for young people. "I hadn't written anything for children. I wasn't really interested. You know? Because I was a poet, I didn't write children's books. I wrote adult poetry," she explains. But babysitting for Cynthia Rylant, a librarian and emerging author, Johnson found herself surrounded by children's books. "For two years I'd pick him [Rylant's son] up from preschool, take him home, and watch him for a few hours." When Rylant began to travel to promote her books, Johnson would stay with her son until she returned.

In college, Maya Angelou was her favorite author. "Maya Angelou was sort of like a goddess to me; she still is. I love her autobiographies. They are incredible. Maya Angelou stood as my idea of what a writer was." As an adolescent, Johnson had been an avid reader, but she read books targeted to adults because young adult literature was still relatively new. So Johnson began to read children's books to Rylant's son, until one day she realized he was playing with his action figures, and she was actually reading to herself and enjoying it. Then something miraculous happened: Johnson picked up the first young adult novel that changed her life, *Sweet Whispers, Brother Rush* by Virginia Hamilton. Johnson had not read literature for youth since junior high, and even then she had never discovered anything like this book. Johnson says, "I just picked up [*Sweet Whispers, Brother Rush*], and I just wept. There were parts of it that floored me." Once again, "book people came to life" for Johnson.[2] In her 2004 Coretta Scott King author award speech, she also credits the work of authors such as Eloise Greenfield, Harper Lee, Carson McCullers, and the Beats for inspiring her.[3]

The second novel for youth that changed Johnson's direction as a writer was Francesca Lia Block's *Weetzie Bat*. While Johnson and Cynthia Rylant sat having coffee, Rylant popped the question: "Okay, where is the young adult novel?" Johnson says she simply looked at Rylant, not sure how to respond. "A few weeks later I heard this knock on my door, and then I heard a car pull off. On my porch I found this book called *Weetzie Bat*. I went, What is this? I read it in an hour or two, and I was like, Wow." From there, Johnson read one young adult book after another until she decided she was ready to write one of her own. She now noticed that her writing had conveyed a youthful voice all along. Now when asked if she will ever return to writing for an adult audience she says, "I'm not interested in adult literature at all—at least not right now."

LEARNING TO WRITE

Without any formal writing courses, Johnson describes her writing ability as natural. However, she says she works hard to hone her craft. "I always believe, and I still believe, that writing is a craft. It's something that you work on; you become better at it as you do it." Deciding to become a nanny rather than a teacher provided Johnson with more time to write. When talking about her writing immediately after deciding to work as a nanny, Johnson says, "I practiced. I quit college, and I just wrote all the time. I knew that being a nanny was going to work for me. The kids would go to school in the morning, and I'd just write all day long." It seemed Johnson had honed her craft to near perfection by the late 1980s. But how did she do it? She simply wrote.

Although Johnson had no published work to her credit, she continued to write. She says, "For most of my life I was a passive participant in my writing. It was something that I did because I didn't have any choice. If I never got anything published, I would still write. I woke up: I wrote poetry. I went to sleep: I wrote poetry."

Initially she attempted to read books about writing but would abandon them after only a few pages. She doesn't go out of her way to form close relationships with writers or attend many conferences either. "I'm not in the society of writers," she says, though she finds them quite interesting. Johnson's writing career is unconventional. She doesn't do many school visits either. In the beginning of her career she felt that school visits would not allow her enough time to write. Now she does more visits but is seriously perturbed when she is sought out during Black History month more rigorously than during the other eleven months in the year. She was also her own agent at one time, negotiating contracts one minute and discussing voice or characterization the next. She soon grew tired of being agent and writer, and, though she was good at both, she turned to the professionals for an agent. She was now free to turn her attention to writing without hindrances.

For her, the learning was in the doing. And if there was a book written that would help her become a better writer, she believed it was a book written for young people. When speaking of deciding to write a young adult novel, she says, "I read YA novels. I never ever read a book about craft. Before I attempted to write a YA novel, I read YA novels for three years. I didn't even attempt to write one because I didn't know the audience." Having ties to a young adult audience is easier for Johnson now that she has a teenage niece and a godson who help her stay familiar with young adult interests. Reading widely in the field and carefully analyzing what makes a book good and how it speaks to young readers also helps Johnson develop her craft. Johnson explains, "How I felt when I was reading *Sweet Whispers, Brother Rush* has everything to do with how I write right now."

For some time, Johnson had been writing what would become *The Other Side: Shorter Poems*. Some of the vignettes were loosely based on people Johnson knew, while lines from others seem influenced by some of her own experiences, though this was probably not intentional. She kept writing the vignettes but turned her attention to picture books as well. As a poet at heart, Johnson found that the precise language of picture books came naturally to her. She begins everything she writes as a poem. Her prose has the cadence and rhythm of poetry. "Everything is written like the beginning of a vignette, and it carries me through," she explains. She continues, "When I start a chapter, I want you to see what's going on. It's all poetry. It's supposed to make you sit up, take notice, and see!" When her first editor, Richard Jackson, speaks of Johnson's ability to use words to evoke visions in the reader's mind, he reminisces about how she creates "striking visual images" and "brilliant pictures" in the opening paragraphs of *Toning the Sweep*: "When Ola found out from the doctor that she was sick and wouldn't get better, she says all she thought about was how she'd miss the color yellow. She went home and cooked a pot of corn on the cob and sliced up three lemons to eat" (*Toning*, 1). Influenced by Frank Polite, an award-winning poet in Youngstown and author of *Letters of Transit*, she believes everything is poetry.

WRITER AT WORK

Johnson describes her writing process as a form of percolating. For her, writing becomes one of those tasks she accomplishes while weeding the garden, taking the bus to her favorite grocery store, or listening to her favorite CDs. She is not one of those writers who gets up early and writes daily as if they are working a nine-to-five job. Johnson says she will never be that type of writer. Instead, she sees herself as undisciplined, only willing to write when inspired—when passion about a topic or issue overcomes her—or forced, when characters appear and demand to be heard. Yet, she has managed to publish at least one title a year since 1989, and she is constantly beginning new projects and completing others. The author never knows when she is going to be inspired or forced to write. "It just happens," she says. There are times when months have passed and Johnson has not written at all, and there are others, like immediately after the death of a close friend, when Johnson could not stop writing. During this period she produced the award-winning *The First Part Last*, *A Cool Moonlight*, and *Bird*.

In her acceptance speech for *The First Part Last* at the 2004 American Library Association conference, Johnson mentioned that she only recently began writing on a computer. "I really hated this computer thing. I didn't have e-mail. I didn't want that much contact with people. I had a fax machine, so I thought that was enough." Now that she has the computer she admits that it makes her job easier. "I waited as long as I could to get into the computer age. Now it's not so daunting." Before she gave in and used a computer, she wrote her manuscripts longhand and typed them on a word processor. Johnson managed to lose a number of manuscripts this way. When she was thirty or forty pages into writing *Toning the Sweep*, her electricity went off, and she lost almost half of the book. Johnson also lost part of her hard copy of *Looking for Red*, but her mother later found it in her home.

Most of the time Johnson writes to music and/or while watching a video. She wrote *Toning the Sweep* while listening to Bob Marley's *Catch a Fire* and watching *Peggy Sue Got Married*. At other times, she writes while young people go in and out of her office. Though she only has two nieces, a nephew, and a few godchildren, many of the children she took care of during her days as a nanny often come to visit. "I'm surrounded by children," she says. In fact, Johnson says her goddaughter, who was twenty-one at the time, sat in her office talking to her while she wrote *A Cool Moonlight*.

When Johnson begins a book, often influenced by something she read in the paper or a suggestion from her editor, Kevin Lewis, she does not know anything about how she will develop the book. She does not outline, use index cards, or employ any of the other methods of invention that "schooled" writers use. In fact, Johnson says she does not know how to outline or use index cards. "When I quit writing on Thursday, I have no idea what I'm going to write on Friday. How I have managed to write novels is amazing to me," she says. Over the years Johnson has grown as a writer despite the fact that her first young adult novel, *Toning the Sweep*, was published with hardly any changes to the original manuscript. She is still developing her skills, especially plot development. "I have serious problems with plot," admits Johnson. She has also learned to self-edit. The author who says, "I am learning as I go," has certainly proven that she is an exceptional writer. In 2005, she was slated as a keynote speaker at the annual Virginia Hamilton conference. Being a three-time winner of the Coretta Scott King author award, 2004 winner of the Michael L. Printz award, and a 2003 recipient of the MacArthur "Genius" grant is only the beginning for this talented writer.

NOTES

1. "Angela Johnson." Retrieved from http://green.upperarlington.k12.oh.us/ohioauthors/johnson,angela.htm on 24 March 2004, 1.

2. "Angela Johnson" in *Contemporary Authors: A Bibliographical Guide to Current Writers in Fiction, General Non-fiction, Poetry, Journalism, Drama, Motion Pictures, Television, and Other Fields, New Revision Series*, vol. 92, ed. Scott Peacock (Boston: Gale Group, 2000), 211.

3. Angela Johnson, "Coretta Scott King Award Acceptance Speech" (unpublished speech given at the annual meeting of the American Library Association, June 2004).

Chapter Two

From Generation to Generation

I've been asked if the characters in my books are actual family members and if the events have truly happened. I answer, No, and smile, for, though I'm extremely close to my family, the thought of putting them in books has never crossed my mind. They are family, you see. They inspire. They disagree. They love. They even behave badly at times. And though you'll never find an actual family member portrayed in one of my stories, their essence drives the characters and are forever an inspiration, which is what I believe it's all about.[1]

Johnson made her debut as a writer of children's picture books in 1989. Author Cynthia Rylant, unbeknownst to Johnson, sent three of Johnson's stories to her editor, Richard Jackson: *Tell Me a Story, Mama*, *Julius*, and *Down the Winding Road*. Jackson recognized Johnson's talent, particularly her knack for developing voice, and decided to find an illustrator for *Tell Me a Story, Mama*. But it would be years before Johnson would receive a call from Jackson concerning the publication of the others. In fact, when Jackson became interested in publishing *Julius*, Johnson had already thrown the manuscript for the book away and forgotten about it, but Jackson had not. Since then, she has published over twenty books for children. Her picture books have won critical acclaim, beginning with her first children's book, *Tell Me a Story, Mama*, which received a Best Books citation from *School Library Journal*. Maria Salvadore applauded the book, claiming that it "validated other families' experiences, regardless of racial or ethnic background."[2] Rudine Sims

Bishop also praised the picture book by describing it as an "impressive debut."[3] In the same *Horn Book* article, Rudine Sims Bishop prophetically dubbed Johnson as possibly one of "the most prominent African American literary artists of the next generation."[4]

From a series of board books about a precocious little boy named Joshua to books that recall events and people of long ago, many of Johnson's picture books are poignant yet lyrical. Most of them focus on family life and include universal themes often found in picture books, such as taking care of a pet (*The Girl Who Wore Snakes* and *Julius*), relocating to another city (*The Leaving Morning*), or adapting to a new babysitter (*Shoes Like Miss Alice's*).

In an article published in *Horn Book Magazine*, Johnson observes:

> Everyone wants family stories to read to their children. And aren't we lucky that there are so many different kinds of families in books so that the children in these families know that there is a place for them? Blended families, racially mixed families, families with gay parents, adopted children, single-parent families, and of course the nuclear family

About her own focus on family she wrote, "I hadn't purposely written my books with a family theme. It was a natural progression of writing what I knew: loving relatives, warm memories of grandparents."[5]

Aunts, uncles, parents, and grandparents are a significant part of Johnson's fiction. She says passionately, "I made a deal with myself a long time ago that no matter what went on in my books, no matter how crazy the situation became, there had to be a grounded adult in the story throwing out a lifeline." This is seen through characters such as Jeff Miller in *Songs of Faith*, who gives Jolette and the other children she befriends hope, and most recently, in *Bird*, as Mrs. Pritchard helps Bird return home. Long before Johnson began to write young adult novels, the adults in her stories served a similar purpose. The adults support, teach, and protect the youth in her books. With few books for children portraying positive images of older people, her books are a much-needed addition to children's and young adult literature.

The aunts in *The Girl Who Wore Snakes* are reminiscent of the aunts in *Toning the Sweep*. Both books were published in 1993. Ali, impressed with Silvia the snake, is the first to volunteer to hold her; as a result, her classmates dub her "the girl who wore the snake." Immediately, Ali becomes attached to the brown, yellow, and orange snake that makes her "think of the sun and the earth and everything in between."[6]

Everyone is puzzled by Ali's interest in snakes, including her parents, but they allow her to make several her pets. Similarly, Ali is surprised when her parents, friends, and teacher are unable to see her snakes' beauty. One day, Ali wraps her colorful snakes around her neck, puts on her backpack, and decides to visit the "old aunts."

Four aunts stand in the doorway looking at Ali; one of them—hand raised in protest—tells Ali that snakes are not allowed in the house. The same aunt wonders about the snakes' diet, while another one calls the snakes "nasty things." The only aunt with a delightful, somewhat giddy facial expression asks to hold one of the snakes, claiming they "remind her of the sun and the earth and everything in between" (*GWWS*, n.p.). This pleases Ali so much that she prances gleefully with snakes wrapped around her arms, neck, and legs. Her aunt's interest in snakes provides her with reassurance. She no longer feels misunderstood. Lucille H. Gregory suggests that the snakes hold a deeper symbolic meaning. She argues that Johnson "indirectly alludes to a parallel between snakes, which elicit an aversion in some people, and African Americans, who are sometimes reacted to in a similar way. But Johnson subverts that irrational bias by transforming the snake into a thing of beauty—an ornament to be admired and worn proudly."[7]

Many of the older characters in Johnson's picture books are men, grandfathers and uncles who are admired by children. The males in Johnson's picture books are reminiscent of strong, sensitive characters in *Heaven* like Marley's biological father, Uncle Jack, and her adopted father, who both love and support her. In *When I Am Old with You*, a young boy with handsome dreadlocks tells his grandfather all of the things they will do together when he is old, while the illustrations show the two engaged in the activities. The rural setting, seen in much of Johnson's work, is vivid and stems from her Southern birthplace and years growing up in rural Ohio. The nameless narrator and his grandfather sit on the porch in rocking chairs, fish in a pond, play cards underneath a tree, eat a picnic lunch, and ride a tractor. Like Emily in *Toning the Sweep*, the boy shares a special relationship with his grandparent that extends out into the community as they wave at passersby and invite friends and neighbors over for a meal.

Community also plays a significant role in *The Rolling Store*. As an African American girl and her white friend make preparations to fill their wagon with treats they hope to sell to neighbors, the girl repeats her grandfather's story about a rolling store that traveled into rural black neighborhoods in Alabama during the early twentieth century. In the end, the grandfather appears just in time to go with the girls to peddle their goods. The community, just as it patronized the rolling store of long ago, comes out to purchase items from the girls. In contrast to the time period that the grandfather's story recalls, the two girls' friendship reflects social change in their contemporary society. Similarly, the community, unlike the historic one depicted in earlier pages of the book, is mixed race. The book conveys Johnson's concern with encouraging cross-cultural relationships, but Johnson surmises that white illustrators of her books often depict culturally diverse supporting characters.

Bonding and learning from elders is a significant part of *Shoes Like Miss Alice's* and *Down the Winding Road*. Oil paintings in rich colors like the royal blue found on each page of *Shoes Like Miss Alice's* convey warmth and confidence, two characteristics Sara needs since her mother is going out and leaving her with Miss Alice, her new caregiver. When the large door closes and Sara is alone with Miss Alice, she considers running after her mother, ignoring Miss Alice, or simply retreating to her room to await her mother's return. Instead, she watches as Miss Alice begins to dance, claiming she is wearing dancing shoes. The dancing becomes contagious, so Sara joins in, forgetting about missing her mother. Dancing makes them hungry, so they have a snack, but then sadness returns. But not for long, because Miss Alice changes her blue shoes to brown ones that she calls her walking shoes. After Sara and Miss Alice "walk in the wind and the leaves,"[8] Miss Alice puts on her soft slippers, her nap shoes, and Sara takes a nap. After naptime Sara forgets to miss her mother because Miss Alice is in her bare feet, and it is time to draw pictures. Soon Mama comes home, Miss Alice is gone, and Sara is dancing around the room in her blue shoes "making believe they were shoes like Miss Alice's." While some critics claimed *Shoes Like Miss Alice's* is warm and heartfelt, at least one critic, Jos N. Holman, noted flaws: "The idea is good, but the story moves slowly and has no real excitement. The writing does not match Johnson's usual superb style of portraying touching human relationships."[9]

Lush green grass, cows grazing, an old red pickup truck, and a tire swing mark the rural setting of *Down the Winding Road*. The protagonist, her brother, and her father visit "the Old Ones," seven aunts and uncles who nurtured her father when he was a boy. The love and support of the Old Ones is showered on the children: "They feed us. And laugh with us."[10] The children develop respect for elders, for their knowledge and their interpretations of history. While the nameless narrator in *When I Am Old with You* thumbs through family photo albums even as old family photos stare at him from the walls, the boy and girl in *Down the Winding Road* look up at the photos of relatives aligned on the walls in the house of the Old Ones. An uncle holds the narrator as her brother Jesse stands at his side. He points at the people—the children's ancestors—in the pictures, teaching them family history. Just as the children learn from the Old Ones in their lives, the Old Ones learn from them and find a sense of joy in sharing their experiences with the young ones.

In *Do Like Kyla*, the narrator adores her big sister, emanating her every move. Johnson says *Do Like Kyla* is a "valentine to Ezra Jack Keats," the white picture-book author said to have been one of the first to write picture books with an African American central character that received mainstream attention.[11] Like Keats's work, many of Johnson's stories depict the happiness of an ordinary day in the lives of African American children. Keats is also one of the authors Johnson read as a child. The picture book is framed so that the initial text is repeated at the end with some variation. The first double-page spread in the book shows two little girls peering out the window. The older sister taps at the window with hopes of gaining the attention of the birds. The younger sister is intrigued by the tapping and decides to try it too. After a day of following her sister's lead, the final illustration serves as a continuation of the first. Once again the two sisters are staring out the window; where in the first picture we only see a medium shot of the girls, the final scene shows them from behind, staring out into the night looking for birds. When they find none, the narrator taps at the window, and her big sister does the same. Though readers cannot see their faces, one imagines the narrator smiling first in surprise and then with satisfaction. The older sister never seems tired of the younger one's interest in what she does. In fact, she seems to encourage it. Similar close-knit sibling relationships are in *Looking for Red*, *Humming Whispers*, and *Heaven*, among others.

The narrator of *The Wedding*, Daisy, admires her older sister as well. In the midst of making wedding plans, Daisy slowly begins to realize that the wedding consists of more than dresses, flowers, and food. The wedding means losing part of her sister as her new husband Jamal "will take sister from me and us and here—but leave them together."[12] *The Wedding* is reminiscent of Carson McCullers's *Member of the Wedding* and Gary Soto's *Snapshots of a Wedding*. The wedding takes on tremendous significance and introduces possibilities of change in the protagonists' lives. Though readers never hear dialogue spoken between the two sisters, the narrator's love for her sister is apparent as pictures and text work together to make this obvious. In the end, Daisy realizes that she is alone and without the immediate attention of her sister, but she still has her parents and the memories of the wedding.

The younger sibling's reliance on parental relationships is shown vividly in *One of Three*. Much of the story focuses on the youngest of three sisters and her relationship with her older siblings. They spend a great deal of time together: walking to school, playing outside their apartment building, taking taxi and subway rides, and shopping with their parents. Though the sisters are loving and supportive of their youngest sibling, there are times when they choose to go places without her. It is at those times when the narrator realizes she becomes a part of a "different kind of three," a set of three that includes her artist parents.

The book's final watercolor painting illustrates the love her sisters, Nikki and Eva, have for her. There is no text on the page. The narrator, tired from reading, painting, and talking with her parents, has fallen asleep on the sofa with a book by her side. One sister sits along the edge of the sofa, leaning in with her elbow propped on her little sister and her hand on little sister's back. Her head is tilted as she watches her sleeping sister. The other sister watches from a different angle. She stands behind the sofa, leaning over it slightly as she looks down on her sister. The image extends the story as it suggests warmth, love, care, and concern. Johnson is also one of three, as she has two younger brothers.

David Soman illustrated most of Johnson's earlier picture books. Richard Jackson says he chose Soman to illustrate *Tell Me a Story, Mama* only after his father, Max Ginsburg, who had illustrated the paperback editions of Mildred Taylor's books, recommended Soman. Critics have praised the way Soman's illustrations contribute to Johnson's stories. Karen James writes of *One of Three*, "Johnson and Soman work well together to capture, on a child's level and without sentimentality, the underlying love and strength of positive family relationships."[13] Johnson gives an enormous amount of credit for the success of her picture books to the illustrators. "I do the easy job," she says.

When asked about her own family relationships, Johnson says, "I have a close family. My parents are still together after over forty years." What about loving siblings? Any sibling rivalry? "I do not have the perfect brother-sister relationship. But my brothers have always been supportive, and we've never had sibling rivalry at all. They would do anything for me. They're annoying at times, but I don't know what sibling isn't." Johnson went on to talk about her position as the oldest sibling and the only daughter. "It's that birth-order thing. I am a little bit more responsible, and I'm tough on them [her brothers] sometimes."

Supportive parents, loving siblings, and strong ties to extended family are a part of what makes *Tell Me a Story, Mama* and *The Leaving Morning* so touching. The protagonist of *Tell Me a Story, Mama* is preparing for bed, but before she goes to sleep she asks Mama to tell her a story. When Mama does not seem to know just the right story to tell, the main character helps her out by suggesting memorable moments from Mama's childhood. As a child, Mama protects her younger sister, convinces her parents to let her have a pet, and is sent to live in St. Louis while her parents work. Johnson refers to her own Aunt Rosetta in the story.[14] Johnson laughs at the memory of her niece as a toddler deeply connected to only two or three stories that she wanted read repeatedly before bedtime. Like her niece, Johnson and her siblings committed their grandfather's stories to memory because they requested them so often.[15] "Kids are always asking their parents to tell me a story, and they want to hear the same story, or they want to read the same book." It is Johnson's sensitive depiction of this familiar experience that touched readers most.

The shadows of two children, brother and sister, holding hands as they stand staring solemnly out the window of an apartment building begin *The Leaving Morning*. The colors of the shadowy illustrations are brown and gray, invoking a dark and somber mood. When the children stand facing the inside of the apartment, the sun has risen, and the light in the room is a mixture of yellowish orange and brown. There are filled boxes all about the room, though pictures of family members still sit perched on coffee tables. The brightness of the next double-page spread signals a flashback as the nameless male narrator describes the lengthy process of packing and preparing to leave. For several brightly colored pages the narrator lists all of the family and friends they said goodbye to. Then, just before they leave the apartment for good, the family—the narrator, who is holding his parents' hands, his older sister, his mother who appears to be pregnant, and his father—are all seated on the floor in the empty apartment attempting to say one final goodbye before they move on to a new place.

As in her fiction for young adults, Johnson often incorporates historical moments into her picture books. In *Toning the Sweep*, it was a glimpse of the Civil Rights Movement. Johnson seemed to suggest in a manner somewhat similar to Toni Morrison's *Love* that members of the black community did not perceive the Civil Rights Movement in a monolithic way.[16] In *Heaven*, amidst the story of a young girl's search for personal identity, Johnson manages to squeeze in another historical moment: the burning of churches in the American South. Conversely, historical moments and figures take center stage in some of her picture books. Johnson dedicates *Those Building Men* to her "wonderful uncle, Johnny Floyd, a building man." It is a poem, accompanied by appealing illustrations, offered as a tribute to all, regardless of race or gender, who, as the note about the book states, "physically labored to build the roads, bridges, railroads, and tall buildings in America."[17] The note goes on to mention storytelling and family history, two concepts that are important across Johnson's oeuvre.

These concepts are certainly a part of *I Dream of Trains* and *Just Like Josh Gibson*. *I Dream of Trains* is set in Mississippi during Reconstruction. The nameless male narrator, the son of a sharecropper, clings to the story of Casey Jones, a famous white engineer who died a tragic death on April 30, 1900.[18] He imagines he is allowed to travel with Casey and his fireman, an African American man named Sim Webb. Casey and his train symbolize hope for the young boy, especially since trains are often linked to notions of freedom and recall the successful abolitionist effort dubbed the Underground Railroad. The boy does not leave Mississippi during the span of the story, but his father suggests that dreaming of trains implies that someday he will leave, hinting at the great migration that found a number of blacks leaving the South for northern states and, they hoped, greater opportunities. This is reminiscent of Johnson's own father's decision to move his family from Alabama to Ohio. Gillian Engberg suggests that young readers "will easily connect with the [protagonist's] deep yearning to escape and the quiet, atmospheric beauty of the language" in *I Dream of Trains*.[19]

Just Like Josh Gibson, as its title suggests, is about another heroic figure who has a number of tall tales attached to his memory. The book combines two stories. Initially, Grandma is busy telling her grand-daughter about the amazing athletic ability of Negro Leaguer Josh Gibson. Then "the story shifts to Grandma's own athletic ability and determination to play baseball 'just like Josh Gibson' despite her gender. It's the 1940s, and girls are not allowed on teams, but one day the Maple Grove All-Stars ask her to fill in, and she helps lead the team to victory."[20] The story is returned to Josh Gibson only in the form of an author's note in the shape of a baseball card that gives details about Gibson's amazing career. *Black Issues Book Review* honored *Just Like Josh Gibson*, calling it as one of the best books of 2004.[21]

Johnson says, "I no longer write the picture books I wrote at the beginning. I now write historical fiction." She credits her editor, author Kevin Lewis, for suggesting that she write historical fiction. When asked about the research involved and the genesis of ideas, again Johnson credited Lewis. He helped her obtain information needed to complete *I Dream of Trains*, and it was his love of baseball, trucks, and trains that has fueled her. Johnson grew up around baseball fans, so writing *Just Like Josh Gibson* came from childhood memories of hearing people talk about him, especially the opening story about Gibson hitting the ball in Pittsburgh and it coming down the next day in Philadelphia. Lewis writes the informative author's notes that conclude most of Johnson's historical fiction. She says Lewis writes them because she finds it difficult to return to a book after she completes it. However, Lewis communicates with her about the importance of the work before drafting the author's note.

Johnson feels her critics have a limited view of her as a writer. She cringed when talking about what critics have dubbed "Angela Johnson books." "It wasn't a mean thing," Johnson says, "but it was a thing that writers don't want to hear." According to Johnson, turning to historical picture books has helped her expand her work. She is at the time of this writing at work on a book about the Tuskegee Airmen to be illustrated by Loren Long, illustrator of Johnson's *I Dream of Trains*, and she has just published *A Sweet Smell of Roses*. Set during the Civil Rights Movement in Selma, Alabama, the book is about two little girls who, without parental supervision, go to a march led by Dr. Martin Luther King, Jr. Though the focus of the book is on the girls and their participation in the march, Johnson said there was talk about making the book appear to be about Dr. King by including his name in the title. Johnson protested for several reasons but mainly because the book is loosely based on two little girls referred to in a segment of *Eyes on the Prize*. In the video, the girls were adults being interviewed about their experiences as youth. According to Johnson, the girls went to the marches without their parents. "The marchers, the adults, took care of them. When the march in Selma turned violent and everyone started running, Albernathy, or one of the others, picked one of them up and ran with them. I always loved the idea of these two little girls."

In the picture book, the girls, in beautiful illustrations rendered in charcoal, "slip past Mama's door and out of the house down Charlotte Street." Once the girls are away from the house, they join the marchers as they wait to follow Dr. King. What appear to be excerpts from Dr. King's speeches and emphatic responses from the audience are in bold type. Once the march has ended, Dr. King has spoken, and freedom songs have been sung, the girls return home to a worried but relieved mother and to the "sweet smell of roses all through [the] house."[22]

Johnson says, "What people fail to realize is that many of those young people went to the marches with their parents standing in the door saying, Don't go." Johnson's statement brings to mind her depiction of Ola in *Toning the Sweep*. Ola chooses not to play a vocal role in the Civil Rights Movement; instead, she takes her daughter across the country to California in an effort to protect her. Johnson says that oftentimes media depicts this era in a romantic light, ignoring the complexity of larger issues. Johnson's parents have shared stories with her about their own experiences during the Civil Rights Movement; their experiences helped develop Johnson's understanding of this period in history.

Martha V. Parravano says *A Sweet Smell of Roses* is "romanticized idealism" and argues that the girls' participation in the march without immediate adult supervision "feels artificial." She does admit, however, that the "pervasive smell of roses is an effective metaphor for the scent of freedom in the air, and Johnson's poetic text is powerful."[23] Parravano and other critics praise Velasquez's illustrations. Johnson is also pleased with the illustrations. She is particularly fond of his use of red, which connotes an odd mixture of beauty and danger, in the stripes on the American flag, the ribbon that adorns the girl's teddy bear, and the roses planted in Mama's window box.

Environmental concerns and the importance of preserving nature make their way into Johnson's board books *Mama Bird, Baby Birds* and *Joshua by the Sea*, just as these issues are also seen in *Toning the Sweep*, *Heaven*, *The Other Side: Shorter Poems*, and a number of her other picture books. For instance, in *Down the Winding Road*, the idea of industrialization destroying the environment is briefly explored. The Old Ones tell the children stories about the trees and remark, "and wasn't it sad when they cut down the old-growth trees around here to put up more highway?"[24]

Identity formation and the importance of individuality can be seen in characters as different as Shoogy (*Heaven*), Ali (*The Girl Who Wore Snakes*), and Violet (*Violet's Music*). Though *Violet's Music* received mixed reviews, most critics seemed to agree that Johnson's point is well taken: cherish your individuality, and do what you love even when others do not understand you. Repeatedly, Johnson's work speaks to readers who are different, assuring them that their differences do not make them inferior.

Reading picture book after picture book, spending time with young people, and recalling moments from her own childhood helps Johnson write picture books her readers love. Johnson remembers the controversy that surrounded *Don't Let the Pigeon Drive the Bus* but ignores it, deciding to focus on the aspect of the book that made it stand out to young readers and to Caldecott judges. Johnson chuckles as she recalls sitting in a mall parking lot reading the book with her mother. Johnson argues that books on writing craft cannot teach her how to write a book that appeals to children; she insists that only reading quality picture books can do that. "Why do kids like *Julius*?" she asks. "Because there is a pig in the house!" This pig brings to mind the phrase parents often use when referring to children's bedrooms: This place is a pig sty! Johnson says children are drawn to stories that "speak to the essence of what [they] understand." This remains at the forefront of Johnson's mind when she writes for young people.

Johnson says, "I didn't think I was going to ever write novels. I thought I would just write picture books for the rest of my life." But in 1993, Johnson proved to her fans and to herself that she could go beyond picture books. Richard Jackson says, "Angie is such an extraordinary writer. I thought older children should be able to read her words and also get her sense of what it's like to grow up in this country."[25]

Mary Helen Washington says, "Writers speak to other writers. They change, challenge, revise, and borrow from other writers so that the literary tradition might well look like a grid in one of those airline magazines that shows the vast and intricate interweaving patterns of coast-to-coast flight schedules."[26] This type of intertexuality between Johnson's literature for young adults and black women's literature written for an adult audience will be explored in the remaining chapters. Readers will note that I have not included her two middle-grade novels, *Maniac Monkeys on Magnolia Street* and *When Mules Flew on Magnolia Street*.

NOTES

1. Angela Johnson, "Family Is What You Have," *Horn Book Magazine* 73, no. 2 (March/April, 1997), 179–80. Academic Search Premier. 4 June 2004. Keyword: Johnson, Angela.

2. Maria Salvadore, "Making Sense of Our World," *The Horn Book Magazine* (March/April, 1995), 230.

3. Rudine Sims Bishop, "Books from Parallel Cultures: New African-American Voices," *The Horn Book Magazine* (September/October, 1992), 620.

4. Rudine Sims Bishop, "Books from Parallel Cultures," 616.

5. Johnson, "Family Is What You Have," 179.

6. Angela Johnson, *The Girl Who Wore Snakes* (New York: Orchard Books, 1993), n.p. (hereafter cited as *GWWS*).

7. Lucille H. Gregory, "Angela Johnson," *Twentieth-Century Children's Writers*, 4th ed., ed. L. S. Berger (Detroit: St. James Press, 1995), 494.

8. Angela Johnson, *Shoes Like Miss Alice's* (New York: Orchard Books, 1995), n.p. (hereafter cited as *MA*).

9. Jos N. Holman, "Review of *Shoes Like Miss Alice's*," *School Library Journal* (July, 1995), 64.

10. Angela Johnson, *Down the Winding Road* (New York: DK Publishing, 2000), n.p. (hereafter cited as *WR*).

11. Carolyn S. Brodie, "Angela Johnson: A Conversation with an Award-Winning Author," *School Library Media Activities Monthly* 17, no. 10 (June 2001): 44.

12. Angela Johnson, *The Wedding* (New York: Orchard Books, 1999), n.p.

13. Karen James, "Review of *One of Three*," School Library Journal (October, 1991), 98.

14. Barbara Thrash Murphy, *Black Authors and Illustrators of Books for Children and Young Adults: A Biographical Dictionary*, 3rd ed. (New York: Garland Publishers, 1999), 209.

15. "Children's Author Donates Book Profits," *Call and Post* 77, no. 6 (January 16, 1992). Retrieved from http://proquest.umi.com.proxy.lib.ohio-state.edu on 18 March 2005.

16. Adam Langer, "Star Power," *Book* (November/December 2003), 40–46.

17. Angela Johnson, *Those Building Men* (New York: Blue Sky Press, 2001), n.p.

18. Angela Johnson, *I Dream of Trains* (New York: Simon & Schuster Books for Young Readers, 2003), n.p.

19. Gillian Engberg, "Review of *I Dream of Trains*," *Booklist* (October 1, 2003), 328.

20. KaaVonia Hinton, "Review of *Just Like Josh Gibson*," *Lansing State Journal* (May 9, 2004), 8E.

21. "*BIBR* Best of 2004," *Black Issues Book Review* (November/December 2004), 32–33.

22. Angela Johnson, *A Sweet Smell of Roses* (New York: Simon & Schuster Books for Young Readers, 2005), n.p.

23. Martha V. Parravano, "Review of *A Sweet Smell of Roses*," *The Horn Book Magazine* 81, no. 1 (January/February 2005), 79.

24. *WR*, n.p.

25. Richard Jackson, Richard Jackson Imprints—Atheneum, telephone interview with the author 2 December 2004 (hereafter cited as Jackson).

26. Mary Helen Washington, ed., *Black-Eyed Susans/Midnight Birds: Stories by and about Black Women* (New York: Doubleday, 1990), 7.

Chapter Three

"Short Takes"

I'm very spare in my writing. I'm not descriptive at all. I believe it's the things left unsaid that are more important to me. I know people who can give you a 400-page book with nothing but description. I'm not that person. I've never written a book literally over 120 pages. If it's over 120 pages, it's because the publishing house stretched the page content.

Johnson's "short takes" are her anthologized short stories and poems, her collection of short stories titled *Gone from Home: Short Takes*, and *The Other Side: Shorter Poems*, her book of poetry. It is here that the author's range becomes clear. For Johnson, writing short stories is a joyful experience. She says they begin as vignettes or character sketches that she extends. The subject matter of many of Johnson's anthologized short stories differs from that of her earlier young adult novels. Some of the main characters are slightly older, many of them experimenting with sex for the first time. The stories are often poetic, honest, and sincere. To date, Johnson has written seven anthologized short stories and is working on an eighth short story to be published in a book of stories about phobias edited by Donald Gallo. Johnson says, "I never would have thought of writing a story on a phobia. It's actually kind of interesting and funny. I'm going to be writing a story on this kid who has a fear of string." The story is titled "D'arcy" because the protagonist, J, is in love with a young lady named D'arcy who gets excited when she hears J will be joining her weaving class. There is only one problem: J's fear of string, which began as the result of a tragic accident that killed his mother. His mother's death is not the focus of the story; however, his feelings about string and D'arcy are.

"Tripping over the Lunch Lady" is a similarly lighthearted and funny story. Nicknamed Jinx, the central character is "an accident waiting to happen." This kid, who frequently hurts herself and others while doing rudimentary tasks such as walking, decides she is going to be a square dancer. When the gym teacher, Mr. Deimeister, has an accident of his own, he leaves lesson plans instructing the substitute to teach square dancing. As she recovers in the hospital a few floors away from Mr. Deimeister, the protagonist realizes she will never be a square-dance champion.

Johnson likes to write stories in response to an editor's request for short prose on a particular theme. She says, "I love doing the stories because it takes me so far out of what I normally do. I love taking directions. I love the creation. I love honing it and making it workable, making it palatable. Creation is wonderful!"

Issues around class, human rights, friendship, love, and diverse family units are echoed throughout her stories. Johnson's earliest short story for young adults, "Flying Away," was published in *But That's Another Story: Famous Authors Introduce Popular Genres* (1996). A slightly altered form of "Flying Away" appears in Johnson's *Gone from Home: Short Takes*. The visually impaired narrator describes his mother's erratic preoccupation with moving from city to city, never really feeling content anywhere. She passes her unsettled nature on to her two oldest children, who leave the family's temporary home in Kansas for California.

Johnson published "Watcher," "Through a Window," and "Atomic Blue Pieces" in three different anthologies in 2001. "Watcher" appeared in Michael Cart's *Love & Sex: Ten Stories of Truth*. Up until Johnson accepted the invitation to contribute to Cart's anthology, her treatment of male-female relationships had been mostly platonic. Even obvious boy-girl relationships such as the one in *Humming Whispers* between Nicole and Rueben seemed to be devoid of sexuality and had the appearance of a relationship between siblings. One of my students, a black male self-proclaimed reluctant reader who chose to read *Toning the Sweep* because of the length, was quite surprised when he connected with it on a personal level. He was convinced that Emily and David Two Starr were only pretending to be close friends and that the final chapters of the novel would reveal that they both wanted to develop an intimate relationship.

Johnson's cautious approach to incorporating themes around sexuality in her work is not uncommon. A number of the stereotypes used to describe African American women are related to sexuality. Since the slave narrative of Harriet Ann Jacobs, this has been a difficult but necessary subject to approach in black women's writing. In "Sweetness," the opening short story in Johnson's collection, *Gone from Home: Short Takes*, lesbian themes are suggested. "[Sweetness] only got real upset when her mom said God wouldn't like her loving another girl" (*Gone*, 17).

Johnson argues that prior to writing short stories such as "Watcher" and "A Kind of Music" her characters simply weren't old enough for themes around sexual relationships—heterosexual or homosexual. *The First Part Last* soon followed, and it is Bobby and Nia's love, intimacy, and sexual encounters that fuel much of the story's conflict, an unwanted pregnancy. The couple continues to have sex even after Nia is pregnant. It is also suggested that Bobby's friends are sexually active but are more concerned about using contraceptives than Bobby and Nia are. Johnson says, "My characters are getting older now, and definitely sex will be an issue." Johnson is at work on two novels at the time of this writing, and she says that teen sexuality is a major theme in both of them.

"Watcher" takes the reader inside the head of a young man experiencing love and sex for the first time. Johnson says, "I've often wondered about the intensity of adolescent love. . . . As there is nothing like first love, what about a first love and a first sexual encounter all rolled into one?"[1] The protagonist's love for Jacks drives him near obsession as he watches her throughout the story, claiming, "She is my religious experience."[2] The protagonist watches people, however, long before he meets Jacks, who, ironically, has been watching him as he moves about Cleveland. Soon the two meet, become inseparable, and the narrator develops all of the symptoms of love sickness: he can't eat, sleep, or stop thinking of Jacks. Like many of Johnson's characters, Jacks is an orphan, caught up in foster homes and then placed with extended family, godmother Ruth, the name Johnson ascribes to Pearl's distant mother in "Home." The description of the two having sex is sensual and loving:

> There wasn't anyone else in the world but me and her. After a while I didn't
> know where her body stopped and mine started. . . . We were stumbling and

touching each other in a cloud, with the sun just burning up the city. And I was thinking I could just die, lying across her smooth skin as long as she would let me.[3]

The two seem to grow closer though Jacks often resides in a place the protagonist cannot seem to reach. Thus, he implies that he watches Jacks for fear of losing her.

Friendships between girls are an essential part of Johnson's work. However, platonic friendship between girls and boys seems to be just as important as noted in *Toning the Sweep* in the form of a platonic relationship between Emily and David. The essence of friendship across gender is portrayed in "Through A Window," which was published in *On the Fringe*. The narrator, Nia, describes her friendship with Nick Gorden, a quiet boy most of the students at school seemed to ignore. Because Nick appeared to be happy, no one, including Nia, suspected that he would hang himself from a stairwell outside his school's chemistry lab. When he does, Nia has a difficult time accepting his death. Both Nia and Nick were outsiders, invisible to those around them but for different reasons. Nia believes her classmates purposefully ignore her. When they do not, they tease her because she has acne, has "non-existent fashion sense," and is the smartest girl in her class. The theme of invisibility seen in a number of Johnson's short stories, particularly in "A Summer's Tale" and "Home," in *Gone from Home*, takes a tragic turn here. At the end of the story, Nia is looking through a window in the Sarah Elizabeth Hollcomb Psychiatric Clinic for Adolescents, not unlike the window from which she witnessed the paramedics taking Nick's body out on a stretcher in the beginning of the story. When Nia recalls her relationship with Nick, including details about his personality, motifs familiar to Johnson's readers surface. The most notable is Nick's preoccupation with the memory of his uncle who died in Vietnam. Of her intentions, Johnson says she was interested in exploring "the unanswerable questions that float around when a seemingly content young person takes their life" and "what happens to a friend left behind . . . who was unable to do anything about it."[4]

Loss is also a significant part of "Atomic Blue Pieces," which appears in *The Color of Absence: 12 Stories about Loss and Hope*. A nameless narrator who mourns the loss of her brother Leon describes the events that led him to run away from home. Leon plays the drums on top of an abandoned building in the Chalky Trailer Park where his family lives until he is framed for a crime he did not commit. T-Boy James, a neighborhood juvenile delinquent, had decided he would seek revenge on people in the community whom he believed turned him in to authorities. He set the building across from the narrator's trailer on fire and left the gasoline can underneath her home. Since Leon believed people in the community would think he set the fire, he hitchhiked out of town, leaving his mother and the narrator forever.

In 2002, Johnson's "A Kind of Music" was one of eleven stories published in *One Hot Second: Stories about Desire*. The short story in verse details a romance between the narrator and Tank, a sensitive young man who says he wants to become a teacher. Though the narrator's mother worries she will become pregnant, she tries to inform her daughter about safe sex by leaving condoms and a copy of *Our Bodies, Ourselves* in her room. The narrator is all too aware of the consequences of unprotected sex, as she has noticed several pregnant girls at school who are younger than she is. When she has sex with Tank, she compares their individual approaches to lovemaking in terms of genres of music. While she considers herself to be "slow R&B," Tank is labeled "funky hip-hop."[5] The importance of supportive parents and making informed choices is evident in this story.

Johnson says, "I think not having sex in young adult literature is tantamount to closing your eyes while driving on the freeway. Teens have sex. Period. Anyone who respects them and wants to tell a realistic story they can relate to acknowledges this fact and portrays all aspects of teen sexuality in its confusing, wonderful, frightening, romantic, dysfunctional, passionate, and sometimes tragic way." Johnson's short stories that focus on teen sexuality do just that.

In "Our Song," intergenerational love and understanding is expressed, connecting it thematically to *Toning the Sweep*. Ole Ma's song is as familiar and comforting to Josie as excelling in sports and outrunning boys. Josie's connection to Ole Ma's Senegalese roots is what is unfamiliar until the family decides to take a trip to Senegal. While there, Josie gains a greater sense of who her grandmother is and of her own growing interest in family traditions, traditions that she hopes to pass on to her own children some day. Similar to "Our Song," other stories by Johnson challenge, or at least question, gender stereotypes. Johnson's choice of female character names (e.g., Jacks, Nic, Rey), interests, and ability to succeed at tasks traditionally associated with masculinity suggest that she recognizes gender as a social construction.

While in high school, Johnson visited northern Africa though she longed to see west Africa where many of the Africans brought to the Americas were taken. Of the trip she says, "I always felt I missed something. There was a longing to see, hear, and feel what I had been raised to believe was my family's true homeland."[6]

GONE FROM HOME: SHORT TAKES (1998)

As the title implies, most of the stories in Johnson's collection deal with youth who live difficult lives and have equally difficult decisions to make about their place in the world. The topics are tough, and the twelve "short takes" pack a deliberate punch. The opening story features a whimsical character named Sweetness. After saving the life of an abandoned baby, ten-year-old Sweetness robs a convenience store at gunpoint, taking only "one hundred dollars and a box of candy bars."[7] But that's only one side of Sweetness. There are others: the one who dances to Motown with her best friend Reyetta for "two straight hours," the one who carries groceries for the elderly, and the one who plays dress up (*Gone*, 14). Johnson vividly conveys her complexity. She is innocent, misguided, confused, and searching. Despite the numerous sides to her personality, Sweetness seems destined to return to being an armed robber, destined to die young. Like most of Johnson's work, the story contains very little dialogue, but what is present is crisp and realistic and helps to move the story forward in some cases and crystallize characterization in others.

Johnson says *Gone from Home* was written during an extremely cold winter when she was still working with Richard Jackson. That particular winter she did not want to write a novel, so she decided to write a collection of stories instead. The stories were influenced by stories in newspapers and on television.[8] She insists that *Gone from Home* is one of her favorite books.

Black women writers such as Gwendolyn Brooks, Alice Walker, and Toni Morrison often write about communities, focusing particularly on how members organize against social ills. This idea is central to "Barn." The story's opening introduces Walter Hamilton, a juvenile delinquent fascinated with barns. Living in urban Ohio, Walter frequently takes trips to the country to study barns and the rural culture. Beginning with its title, the story elicits questions, many of which go unanswered. Why is Walter obsessed with barns, and why is the narrator simultaneously afraid and enamored of Walter when he speaks? Many of the stories in the collection call for a certain measure of disbelief. "Barn" is certainly one of them. It is difficult to believe that Walter is able to entice, with very little effort, the young city dwellers to take a trip to the country at five o'clock in the morning to explore barns. The narrator's motive is clear: she is in love, but what about the others? They are shadowy stock characters whom readers may never know. They listen tentatively as Walter lectures them about farm life and how barns are monuments to a forgotten, distant era. When they all return, they are converted, as their eyes narrow and look differently at urbanization. Johnson uses carefully chosen details to contrast urban and rural settings. The wine bottles, crack vials, and inner-city crime are repulsive. The narrator remembers Walter's hysteria when his cousin is murdered. Characters begin to speak of the Native Americans who once lived uninhibited on the land as they head for the subway station.

Why does this story work? Because readers like what Walter is trying to do. He is a prophet of some sort, wanting to change the world but unsure as to how. He reminds readers of themselves—or at least of the self they would like to become. "Soul" works in a similar way. The message in "Barn," and in Johnson's other work, is clear: industrialization, urbanization, and capitalism often has an adverse impact on traditional core values.

Greg and Mick, the main characters of "Soul," have been friends since preschool. They are animal-rights activists, of sorts, but in the beginning of the story Johnson continues to explore the antiwar sentiment found in *Songs of Faith* and *The Other Side*. "War is bad," Mick concludes after reading about the French and Indian War. A kitten that Greg finds asleep on his bed turns out to be the first of a number of animals Mick and Greg rescue from pet stores. Mick feels that animals have souls and that it is inhumane to cage and sell them, as soulless humans do. They give the animals to people who want to take care of pets, like Mick's neighbor whose bulldog has recently died. Though Mick and Greg are not caught, their deeds do not go unnoticed. An article about the missing animals appears in the paper, suggesting that the thieves are "sickies, sacrificing the poor pets for some cult" (*Gone*, 90). This hurts Mick, so he writes a letter to the paper denouncing the accusation, and their efforts to save animals are halted for a while, until they eventually decide they have freed enough animals or at least made a profound point to members of their community.

Social issues and activism are also explored in "A Summer's Tale." The story focuses on a girl's curiosity about a seemingly homeless man who collects egg cartons. With the gift of a six-pack of beer on an uncomfortably hot day, the protagonist convinces the man to share his story with her. She insists, "everyone's got a story" (*Gone*, 28). His story is whimsical. Twenty years earlier, the man had decided to commit suicide. He had planned to throw his body before a train, but the next train was delayed due to a wreck caused by a ton of eggs littering the tracks. Sensing the delay was fate, the man decided he would continue to live. A cart full of stolen egg cartons reminds him "how strange life is and how dumb, too" (*Gone*, 30).

Many of the stories read like dramatic monologues, as if Johnson has inhabited the characters herself in order to allow them to speak directly to the reader. At least three of the stories are strategically placed throughout the book simply for comic relief. A feisty mother, a clumsy girl, and two bickering but kind-hearted gentlemen make up the cast of characters in one of the shortest stories in the collection, "Bad Luck." The protagonist falls while walking down the street and knocks a tray of flowers out of a man's hands and onto her own head. The man becomes angry, ignores the mess in front of the deli, and argues that the girl and her mother are responsible for the ruined petunias. Before an arrangement is worked out, the man who owns the deli suggests that they clean up the mess in front of his shop. Frustrated, the protagonist attempts to leave the scene but finds when she wakens that she is in a hospital. But before she can take a bite of the pastrami sandwich or enjoy the pot of petunias her mother got from the gentlemen on the street, the hospital bed malfunctions, and she has another accident that damages her back. This story does not seem to complement the collection as much as some of the others do, but it does evoke a chuckle. Each time the narrator's day seems to improve, she has an accident similar to those depicted by comedians who do physical comedy in films and sitcoms. The comic relief is needed as two emotionally drenching tales of loss surround the story.

Most of the stories are about young people who have to leave home either metaphorically or physically, but there is little thought of the ones the protagonist leaves behind. "By the Time You Read This" is different. It is a humorous tale written in the form of a letter that begins like a possible suicide note. "To the Ones I Love" (*Gone*, 64). The letter actually expresses the protagonist's regrets for leaving her hair stylists. Noel and her family are moving to Philadelphia and will probably never see the wonderful people who have saved each of her family members from one fashion emergency after another at the Big Hair and Sharp Nail Design Trough.

Voice, which is central to most of Johnson's work, becomes an issue in "Batgirl," as the protagonist, in a sassy tone, recalls the time she refused to speak. The humorous story describes the confusion generated when a bat bit the protagonist. When Batgirl's friend Keisha sees the bat, she screams, falls into the backseat of a stranger's car, and knocks him in the head. Stunned by the blow, the man speeds off with Keisha in his backseat. Batgirl runs after them, a neighbor calls the police, and then things quickly return to normal.

Difference is a part of the lives of the main characters in "A Handful" and "Flying Away." "A Handful" follows the progression of a hyperactive boy, perhaps with attention deficit disorder, who is afraid of bridges. His brother Kevin creates a story about a flying boy who uses his superhuman powers to provide fun and good times for himself. The story helps the boy pretend he is able to fly over bridges when the family takes trips and have to travel over them. The story, and the fear of bridges, originated when Kevin rescued the boy as he dangled from a bridge near his grandmother's home. Years of being unexplainably rambunctious and kicked out of schools are put to an end when he saves someone's life and passes on the story of the flying boy.

Like Nicole, the mentally ill character in *Humming Whispers*, the narrator's mother in "Flying Away" loves planes and dreams of escaping in one. And similar to the narrator of "A Handful," Victor is special; he is different. The story connects well with Johnson's interest in respect for differences. When he was one year old, Victor lost his hearing and his ability to recall the few words he had learned. Yet he hears his family's thoughts. Though the family uses sign language to communicate with him, he is not confined to signs. Their expressions, actions, and mannerisms are all used to discern their thoughts. He knows that his mother is planning to move the family away again and that his twin siblings, Brother and Cookie, will not be happy about this. The reader realizes

Victor's perceptions are valid when the next scene reveals that the family is sitting in a truck stop. Cookie clings to Brother as she "rolls her eyes at Mama," and Brother refuses to look up from his Coke (*Gone*, 71). As with Shoogy's twin siblings in *Heaven*, Brother and Cookie rely mostly on each other.

This story makes Johnson's picture book titled *The Leaving Morning* seem romanticized. Mama does not give her children the opportunity to say good-bye to friends or to tie up loose ends. As is her custom, she makes all of the arrangements alone and in secret. Repeatedly, Victor suggests that Brother and Cookie "can't understand about the leaving" (*Gone*, 71). Johnson uses repetition to increase the tension between Mama and the twins and to foreshadow the twins' decision to leave the family in Kansas.

Mama lives on a whim, making hasty decisions that uproot the family without concern for repercussions. This story fits neatly into this collection because Mama repeatedly attempts to make a home for herself and her family but finds it difficult because of her own character flaws. "Home is important—even if we have more than three a year" (*Gone*, 76).

The strongest stories are those that deal with mother-daughter (or othermother) relationships such as "Sweetness," "Starr," and "Home." Just as details describing the violent, urban setting in "Sweetness" are partially to blame for the protagonist's tragic end, her strained relationship with her mother is also implicated. Religion prevents Sweetness's mother from being attentive. Sweetness believes God exists and is puzzled and disheartened when she cannot see him. Her mother makes matters worse, insisting that Sweetness "wasn't right with Him" (*Gone*, 15).

Throughout Johnson's work, she critiques organized religion, often suggesting its dangers. Her novels and short stories certainly employ a departure from traditional religious views customarily espoused by some of the members in the African American community. There is a certain degree of negativity attached to the religious views of Jolette's stepmother in *Songs of Faith*. Interestingly, Jolette and Robert choose not to make pacts with God in an effort to change their lives; they make pacts with themselves instead. Skepticism surrounds religion in *Toning the Sweep*, too, and it is even suggested that Emily and her family do not place much faith in God or religion. "I haven't ever prayed to God in my whole life," Emily says (*Toning*, 6). The ritual of toning the sweep suggests a belief in the supernatural rather than in the idea es-poused by Christians: one's soul goes to a final resting place, and it doesn't need assistance. It is Minnie Jacobs, perhaps a type of conjure woman who reads fortunes and talks about ghosts, who introduces the idea of toning the sweep to Emily. In *The Other Side*, religion is pre-sented as restrictive and sterile. The speaker and her friend Kesha have to dance "in the woods 'cause her parents / got saved and didn't allow it" (*Other Side*, 21). Similarly, Miss Annie Morgan finds religion and donates her silk dresses to the Baptist Church (*Other Side*, 15). Like Sweetness, Kesha sinks deeper into sin, convinced that her initial sin is so great that it will separate her from God indefinitely.

Mother-daughter relationships are at the heart of *Toning the Sweep* and *Heaven*, and in both novels mothering is an act that transcends biological connections and includes othermothers. Patricia Hill Collins says that within West African societies "Mothering was not a privatized nurturing 'occupation' reserved for biological mothers."[9] Mothering children was viewed as "a collective responsibility" and a "woman-centered" activity not confined to the biological mother.[10] Thus, we get the West African proverb, "It takes a village to raise a child." In other words, othermothers offer a different dimension to motherhood including both biological mothers as well as other women (or men) within the community who take on the responsibility of rearing children. Echoed throughout Johnson's work is Gloria Joseph's fitting statement that "the concept of motherhood cannot be reduced to a biological function."[11] In *Toning the Sweep*, Ola and Martha act as othermothers. Ola takes care of David and his siblings when she learns their parents abandoned them, while Martha has devoted her life to caring for children with parents who will not or cannot care for them. Both women mother naturally and without question, as if it were expected of them.

Bobby might arguably be described as an othermother. As Feather's primary caregiver, he nurtures her. He is described as having "that cover-them-in-a-soft-blanket thing going on," (*Heaven*, 34), and he often "looks at Feather as if she is the only baby in the whole world" (*Heaven*, 26). Marley recognizes Bobby's look because she has seen it in her own adoptive parents' eyes, particularly her father's. Marley's adoptive father shares a connection with her unlike the one she has with her adoptive mother. It is her father who knows the exact moment he needs to go to her in the middle of the night when she is having a nightmare. It is also her father who hung the stars and the moon on her ceiling and knows exactly which stars to replace when they refuse to shine. Johnson certainly uses the main male characters in both *Heaven* and *The First Part Last* to challenge traditional ideas held about masculinity and innate ability to nurture.

Othermotherhood is uniquely portrayed in *Heaven* in other ways too. Marley does not realize she is being raised by an othermother until she learns that her own mother was killed in a car accident when she was a baby. Much of the novel is devoted to Marley's coming to terms with the notion that a mother does not always share a biological connection, yet Marley looks at her adoptive mother and sees aspects of herself.

Othermothering is loosely defined in "Starr" as well. As an othermother herself who has served as a caregiver in numerous capacities to children not biologically her own, Johnson seems to have a certain affinity and sensitivity for the role. This is clearly seen in "Starr." Nic, the narrator of "Starr," likes snakes, going shopping with her friends, and remembering good times spent with Starr. The first line of the story increases curiosity because it is obvious that Starr is no longer in Nic's life. A few lines later, the flashback begins to answer the reader's questions.

At fourteen years old, Nic argues that she is too old for a babysitter, but her father Jimmy does not listen. The story sounds familiar, almost like a young adult version of Johnson's picture book *Shoes Like Miss Alice's*. Like Miss Alice, Nic's babysitter promises to be unique, fun, and loving. She drives to work on a "mountain bike painted Day-Glo," and her "shaved head, pierced-lip [and] COOK THE RICH SLOWLY T-shirt" baffles Jimmy and amuses Nic (*Gone*, 48). With a Ph.D. in psychology, thirty-two-year-old Starr is probably a dramatized version of Johnson who stopped attending Kent State and decided to become a babysitter/nanny in order to devote more time to developing her writing skills.

It turns out that despite Jimmy's and the narrator's initial reservations, Starr is exactly what their family needs. She becomes an othermother to Nic, offering the love and sentimentality the narrator, whose own mother is dead, had not known she needed. The tone of the story changes when Starr asks a man to read tarot cards. The narrator is overcome with sadness but does not learn why until it is too late. The reader recognizes that Johnson uses the incident to foreshadow difficult times ahead. Slowly, Starr begins to change and decides to take Nic to visit her parents in the desert. It's not clear if they live in Little Rock, California, but their free spirits and unconventional style, and their description as "old hippies who made ceramics and had posters of Malcolm X and Margaret Sanger on their walls," suggest as much (*Gone*).

By the end of the summer, Starr has changed completely and begun to come to terms with her terminal illness. She now wore "[s]imple hair" and the "lip ring was gone, and she was wearing what Jimmy calls adult clothes" (*Gone*, 54). At Venice Beach, Starr pulls her wig off and tosses it at a waiter, reminding Johnson fans of Ola and what her hair meant to her. "My hair is my only vanity" (*Toning*, 47).

There is loss of various kinds throughout the collection of stories, but here Nic loses a mother figure. Johnson uses small details to alert the reader that Starr will soon leave Nic. "Starr had started to spend most of the day looking out the window at the road" (*Gone*, 54). By the story's end, Starr is long gone, and Nic is fifteen. It is summer again, and because she has matured during the year Jimmy tells her she does not need a babysitter. Nic's first reaction is to disagree until finally her growth becomes evident to her.

"Home" includes another mother-daughter relationship, but initially it appears that Ruby is acting as Pearl's othermother. Constance Borab says "the depiction of mothers who failed to live up to their responsibilities" was missing from African American literature, particularly by women, and mothers generally "were not allowed to escape oppression by abandoning their children or even by going insane."[12] Borab maintains that in the sixties and seventies black women writers for adult audiences (e.g., Alice Walker and Toni Morrison) created few "long-suffering, self-sacrificing, ever-patient, church-going black [women] who offer . . . hope and emotional strength to others."[13] In stories like "Home," mothers do the unthinkable: they abandon their children. As in her stance in *Running Back to Ludie*, Johnson tries to remain neutral about this. When Ruby leaves again and Pearl cannot be sure she will return she says, "People leave and come back—or just don't do anything at all" (*Gone*, 43).

Like Bird, Pearl leaves home in search of a parent. She boards a Greyhound bus and pretends to be a boy and does not stop until she has reached The Tides and has found Ruby. She follows Ruby around town as Nicole follows Sophy around in *Humming Whispers*. Pearl wants to know more about Ruby because she suspects that she is her mother, though the two do not make maternal connections explicit. Just when Pearl is getting to know Ruby, she abandons her again, but this time she promises that she will return. Mother-daughter relationships are not the only theme in the story. The story is also another indictment against urban society and the way in which the poor are invisible. "People in the city are so good at not seeing that I don't even think they know they're blind" (*Gone*, 34). Pearl associates with other young people who are homeless and eat out of the dumpster at Ray's Bar. Pearl says Ray does not believe in homeless youth, and to confirm it he lets them know that he does not like them and locks his dumpster. But Ray's actions do not always support his stance. He puts food he intends to throw in the dumpster by the door of the bar, and often the food is freshly prepared and wrapped.

The plants and flowers described in the final story in the collection, "A Break," sound beautiful though they are meant to characterize the protagonist's mother, Sophia, as eccentric. The scenery is reminiscent of Johnson's own yard. Though she does not have two hundred, she does have a number of flowers in her yard, and many of them look like baby sunflowers but are actually Brown-eyed Susans. The air around her house smells like peppermint, too, thanks to her garden of peppermint plants growing in the backyard. She says she was warned not to plant them in the ground, but she didn't listen, and the peppermint dominated the basil and chives she had planted earlier. Johnson loves to garden, but says she is an undisciplined gardener like Sophia. "I love everything, but when the flowers deplete, I never cut them down."

Sophia loves to garden too, but she is primarily an artist. When the story begins, she has suffered a nervous breakdown and is spending time in a "New Age 'rest home'" (*Gone*, 104). Leafy misses her mother and doesn't quite understand why she frequently leaves her to get rest at the home. When Stickle, Leafy's dog, dies of heart failure and her friend Jamal helps her bury him, her uneasiness increases. Stickle, old like Chico, the dog of Johnson's childhood, seems autobiographical. She says Chico lived to be eighteen or nineteen years old and the family was torn when he died.

Sophia finally comes home and finds Leafy sleeping in the car. Leafy recalls a scene from her childhood similar to the one Marley has in *Heaven*. Unlike Marley, Leafy chooses to hide in the snow, hoping her mother will not find her. Frightened because Leafy is not home, Sophia looks out the window and spots the top of Leafy's red hat. Like Marley's mother, Sophia dashes out into the snow in a slip and pulls Leafy "out of the drift" (*Gone*, 107).

Cornelia Hoogland, a reviewer for the *Journal of Adolescent and Adult Literacy*, gave *Gone from Home* a mixed review, arguing that some of the stories "lift off the page and some are plodding."[14] Further, she implies that the entire collection lacked rigorous editing. In her opinion, two of the weaker stories, "Bad Luck" and "A Summer's Tale," "should have been edited or removed from the collection as they are weak."[15] Nancy Gilson's comments were more favorable, though she calls the stories "intentional puzzles" that leave the reader grasping at loose ends.[16]

Racial identity is obscure in most of the stories, so one can only assume that the characters are African American. Nevertheless, the collection shows Johnson's commitment to advocating for all children, but especially the disadvantaged. In 1992, with only three picture books to her credit, Johnson donated the profits from *Tell Me a Story, Mama*, *Do Like Kyla*, and *When I am Old with You* to the Head Start program she attended. Many of the stories are reminiscent of literature for young people written by June Jordan. Jordan's young characters often live in urban centers and are poor or working class. Like a few of Johnson's characters, Jordan's take pride in their neighborhoods.

THE OTHER SIDE: SHORTER POEMS (1998)

Johnson writes picture books, young adult novels, short stories, and poetry. Ironically, Johnson, who initially saw herself as a poet, has only written one volume of poetry, published after the success of over fifteen picture books and two young adult novels. Johnson fans did not see this other side of her talent until 1998 when a significant amount of the poetry she wrote during her early years as a writer became *The Other Side*: *Shorter Poems*. The book is dedicated "To poets and Windham." Johnson says no one at Windham High School where she graduated understood her poetry. They thought it was too bleak, too negative, so it was never published in any of the school publications. The preface serves as a statement of defense for Johnson's poetic style. "My poetry doesn't sing the song of the sonnets," she maintains, "but then I sing a different kind of music—."[17]

The book received good reviews, though most critics thought, with good reason, that it was autobiographical. At the suggestion of one of her editors, she sent family photos to the publishing company. She was told the photos would be a great addition to the book. At the time she did not realize that people at the publishing company would see the photos and decide that the book was autobiographical. Her editor was out of the country when a copy of the first printing of the book arrived at Johnson's door announcing on the flap that *The Other Side* is autobiographical. Johnson says her first reaction was to panic. But since then, the book has been reprinted, and the flap has been changed. Since the book went on to win the Coretta Scott King Honor Award and the Lee Bennett Hopkins Award and was listed as an NCSS-CBC Notable Children's Trade Book in the Field of Social Studies, Johnson says she has to constantly tell people that it's not autobiographical.

Very few people have heard her. As late as 2000, an article written by Daniel D. Hade with Lisa Murphy, a member and the chair of the 1999 Lee Bennett Hopkins Poetry Award Committee, respectively, assert that Johnson is the protagonist of *The Other Side*:

> The memories of Shorter seem to come flooding back to Johnson. She begins by writing about her grandmother's news that Shorter is being demolished to make a dog track and moves to the scene of homes being destroyed, then shifts to the people she remembers as being part of her life as a young girl living in Shorter.[18]

Shorter, Alabama, does exist. It sits in Macon County, east Alabama, about thirty minutes away from Tuskegee University where Johnson was born in the campus hospital. In 1990, Shorter had a population of about 461, 74 percent of which was African American and 26 percent white.[19] In the second poem, "Pullin' Down Shorter," the speaker's grandmother tells her to return to Shorter "to see your past before it's all dust, baby" (*Other Side*, 2). According to Grandma, Shorter will be pulled down to make room for a dog track. The "dog track" exists too. It is known as the Victory Lane Greyhound Park. However, Shorter was not demolished because of it.

The speaker returns to Shorter to see that the town is virtually deserted. Memories of a childhood lived there flood the speaker's thoughts. She recalls the party her best friend Carla organized to celebrate her move to Ohio. She recalls the places she once frequented such as the Wash-a-Teria, where "Brown babies running 'round in their un-derwear inside," Miss Delta's for piano lessons, and the woods where she used to dance to contemporary music with her friends (*Other Side*, 5). She recalls political issues and certain activists from the community, too. She is especially proud of Uncle Fred, who has a scar on his face given to him by a man who did not want him to order at a lunch counter in Montgomery, Alabama. The incident frightened his mother and nearly forced her to leave the South for good as Ola had done in *Toning the Sweep*.

Yet, it is while living in Cleveland that the speaker of "Nineties" is called nigger for the first time, emphasizing the slow progression of some Americans even long after the Civil Rights Movement and recall-ing Countee Cullen's poem "Incident." Johnson has juxtaposed reactions to the use of the racial slur when she was growing up to the present day. "When I went to school, it [using the word *nigger*] was something that was so incomprehensible. It was something that could totally quiet three thousand people. Suddenly the '80s started happening, and I was around teenagers who said they hear the word five or six times in the hallway at school. I was appalled."

The speaker's cousin in *The Other Side* is an ex–Black Panther who "could stare down / a killer" (*Other Side*, 40). Mama's friend, Nickie Jones, sounds like Angela Davis. She hides out from the FBI in Shorter until someone, angry because Nickie's husband is a Republican, turns her in. The images of ordinary people the speaker once knew loom just as large as the hometown legends: Miss Pearl, an immigrant from Ja-maica; Miss Annie Morgan, an entrepreneur; Harper Crew, a storyteller; and Mr. Crawford Fisher, arguably the oldest man in Shorter, are all memorable. Some of the poems, like "Smoking with T. Fanny," are hu-morous. Grandma's unconventional methods of disciplining the speaker and T. Fanny—she locks them in a broom closet and demands that they smoke an entire pack of unfiltered cigarettes—ensure that the girls will never view smoking as glamorous again.

The poem "Walter" (the same name as the protagonist of one of the short stories in *Gone from Home*) brings to mind her short story "Atomic Blue Pieces" published in James Howe's *The Color of Absence: 12 Sto-ries about Loss and Hope*. Walter, trying to avoid being a ward of the state, is seen hitchhiking out of Shorter. Recalling the incident, it be-comes obvious that the speaker continues to feel a sense of loss due to

Walter's absence in her life. At fourteen years old, she has looked back
on her short life and grown from her reflection. As Hade and Murphy
write, the book embodies the importance of memory, "the memory of being somewhere, a place that has shaped [the speaker] into the woman
[she's] become."[20] Themes familiar to Johnson readers, such as the ef-
fect of World War II on the black community, oppression, discrimination, and heroic leaders, are all in Johnson's thin volume of poetry.

OTHER POEMS

Johnson has also published poems in several anthologies including the
Coretta Scott King Book Award–winning *In Daddy's Arms I Am Tall:
African Americans Celebrating Fathers* in which she juxtaposes the
hands of the female speaker's father which were "hard and callused"
during the work week, "But on Sundays, / those hands, you see / felt
soft, / and would hold my mama's and walk her to church, / Quietly."[21]
Set in Alabama, the poem, similar to *The First Part Last*, conveys both
black male strength and sensitivity.

Conversely, "From Above," a part of Jan Greenberg's *Heart to Heart:
New Poems Inspired by Twentieth-Century American Art*, is a poetic response to Faith Ringgold's acrylic on canvas painting *Tar Beach*.[22] Similar to some of Johnson's more recent work, and reminiscent of Ringgold's picture books, the theme of flying is central to the poem.

"A Girl Like Me," published in Asher's *On Her Way: Stories about
Growing Up Girl*, is reminiscent of a poem in Johnson's *Running Back
to Ludie* titled "Super Girl."[23] The flying motif well established in
"From Above," and in short stories such as "Flying Away," is also
echoed as the speaker dreams of flying, a type of Supergirl who is always "thinking up high and making everything better than the
dream."[24]

NOTES

1. Angela Johnson, "Watcher," in *Love & Sex: Ten Stories of Truth*, ed.
Michael Cart (New York: Simon & Schuster, 2001), 192.

2. Johnson, "Watcher," 184.

3. Johnson, "Watcher," 188.

4. Angela Johnson, "Angela Johnson," in *On the Fringe*, ed. Donald R. Gallo (New York: Dial, 2001), 74.

5. Angela Johnson, "A Kind of Music," in *One Hot Second: Stories about Desire*, ed. Cathy Young (New York: Alfred A. Knopf, 2002), 212–13.

6. Angela Johnson, "Angela Johnson," in *Memories of Sun: Stories of Africa and America*, ed. Jane Kurtz (New York: Amistad, 2004), 252.

7. Angela Johnson, *Gone from Home: Short Takes* (New York: DK Publishing, 1998), 11 (hereafter cited as *Gone*).

8. Brodie, "A Conversation with an Award-Winning Author," 44.

9. Patricia Hill Collins, "The Meaning of Motherhood in Black Culture and Black Mother-Daughter Relationships," in *Double Stitch: Black Women Write about Mothers & Daughters*, eds. Patricia Bell-Scott et al. (Boston: Beacon Press, 1991), 45.

10. Collins, "The Meaning of Motherhood in Black Culture and Black Mother-Daughter Relationships," 45.

11. Gloria Joseph and Jennifer Lewis, *Common Differences: Conflicts in Black and White Feminist Perspectives* (Garden City, New York: Anchor Press/ Doubleday, 1981), 83.

12. Constance Borab, "Freeing the Female Voice: New Models and Materials for Teaching," in *Teaching African American Literature: Theory and Practice*, eds. Maryemma Graham, Sharon Pineault-Burke, and Marianna White Davis (New York: Routledge, 1998), 86.

13. Borab, "Freeing the Female Voice: New Models and Materials for Teaching," 86.

14. Cornelia Hoogland, "Review of *Gone from Home: Short Takes*." *Journal of Adolescent and Adult Literacy* 43, no. 5 (February 2000), 502.

15. Hoogland, "Review of *Gone from Home: Short Takes*," 502.

16. Nancy Gilson, "Prolific Author Appeals to all Youths," *Columbus Dispatch* (February 25, 1999). Retrieved from http://shop.dispatch.com/ newsarchive/ArchiveList.asp on 4 August 2004.

17. Angela Johnson, *The Other Side*: *Shorter Poems* (New York: Orchard, 1998), xii (hereafter cited as *Other Side*).

18. Daniel D. Hade with Lisa Murphy, "Voice and Image: A Look at Recent Poetry," *Language Arts* 77, no. 4 (March 2000), 350.

19. Retrieved from http://www.townofshorter.com/history.html on 15 July 2004.

20. Hade and Murphy, "Voice and Image: A Look at Recent Poetry," 351.

21. Angela Johnson, "Her Daddy's Hands," in *In Daddy's Arms I Am Tall: African Americans Celebrating Fathers*, illustrated by Javaka Steptoe (New York: Lee & Low Books, Inc., 1997), n.p.

22. Angela Johnson, "From Above," in *Heart to Heart: New Poems Inspired by Twentieth-Century American Art*, ed. Jan Greenberg (New York: Harry N. Abrams, Inc., 2001), 25.

23. Angela Johnson, "A Girl Like Me," in *On Her Way: Stories about Growing Up Girl*, ed. Sandy Asher (New York: Dutton Children's Books, 2004).

24. Angela Johnson, "A Girl Like Me," 4–5.

Chapter Four

Discovering Oneself[1]

"Every day it all gets more fuzzy around the edges about the people who call themselves our families," Marley, the protagonist of *Heaven*, decides.[2] In African American communities the line between family and friends is often blurry, as fictive kin join with biological relatives to form a family unit. The importance of family networks, particularly sibling relationships, family history, and one's unique place within its structure is at the center of much of Johnson's work. Family dynamics, including othermothers and fictive kin, in particular, are a significant part of two of her earlier novels, *Toning the Sweep* and *Heaven*. Each protagonist of the two Coretta Scott King Book Award winners must look to her family for answers to her deepest questions about herself.

TONING THE SWEEP (1993)

When *Toning the Sweep* begins, the protagonist, Emily, has written a letter to Ola, her unconventional grandmother, after learning that Ola has cancer and will move from Little Rock, California, to Cleveland, Ohio, to live with Emily and her parents. The letter establishes the nature of her relationship with her grandmother and expresses her concern for Ola and her eagerness to help her feel better. Emily's letter also tells of her defiance, a common characteristic found in Johnson's protagonists. While Doreen in *Songs of Faith* spray paints the bicentennial signs in an effort to resist the celebration of nationhood during a time when black soldiers who fought in the Vietnam War were not truly free, Emily refuses to see the relevance of pledging allegiance to the U.S. flag. Emily's defiance foreshadows the upcoming themes of injustice and inequality Johnson intends to suggest later in the novel. Emily's refusal to salute the flag, an emblem of freedom and justice, signals the insecurity of black citizenship in the United States, especially during the 1960s when Emily's grandfather was the target of a racially motivated crime. On the plane en route to California, Diane, Emily's mother, decides it is time that she talk to Emily about her grandfather's death, uncovering parts of the family's past.

Sharing this information helps propel Emily toward an understanding of who she is and what she is capable of accomplishing. Learning who her elders are and were is one of the ways Emily can discover her sense of self. Right away she takes this task on, believing that she must accomplish it alone. She says, "Haven't really done much by myself . . . I should find out everything about Ola on my own," (*Toning*, 22). Behind the video camera, Emily learns several shocking truths about her family history, including the source of her mother's bitterness toward Ola and her feelings about the desert. As time progresses, Emily learns more family history that connects her to her grandparents and mother.

In much of Johnson's work family members who see each other daily slowly realize they have much to learn about one another. Emily is quite surprised when she hears her mother praying. Emily thinks, "I didn't know that Mama believed in God until I heard her in the bathroom in the airport praying," (*Toning*, 5–6). She soon learns that there is more about her mother that she does not know. While talking to Sally Hirt, she learns that when she was fourteen years old Diane found her father's dead body in the woods and never fully recovered from the discovery. Johnson says Diane's father was lynched, but her sparse writing doesn't make this detail explicit. Emily says her grandfather was shot "by the side of his car," but the fact that Diane finds his body in the woods suggests that he might have been lynched (*Toning*, 35). Diane blames her father's death on the family's failure to participate in the Civil Rights Movement. When asked about this, Johnson says, "These are the other stories. [This era] was much more complicated. Life wasn't television. People weren't good and evil. You had blacks who marched in the street and those who said This doesn't have anything to do with me; this isn't going to make any difference." Johnson continues, "Ola's fight was a personal thing. She ended up living her life the way she wanted to live it, and she didn't think she could do that where she was."

The strength found in "family outside of . . . family" is expressed as members of Ola's community, particularly Martha and the aunts, act as family members (*Heaven*, 128). The depiction of the beauty of friendship between adult women comes from Johnson's own experiences. While young, she admired the women in her family and their female friends as they sat together telling stories. Johnson recalls her excitement as a child when she learned that one of her aunt's friends was "going to a commune and another was going backpacking through the country." According to Helen Washington, black women writers "emphasize this concern with female bonding and suggest that female relationships are an essential aspect of self-definition for women."[3]

Similarly, Lorranine Bethel describes the bond between women-friends as: "emotionally intense, . . . [an] integral . . . part of the black community."[4] Ola, the aunts, and Martha form a network of women-friends who garden, quilt, and tell stories. They are courageous and strong, carving out places for themselves in a society in which they are disenfranchised because of race and gender. Emily takes pride in them all, but especially in Ruth as she recalls that Ruth "was one of the first women to work on a road crew" (*Toning*, 40).

The women encourage Emily in other ways too, such as in their unwillingness to adhere to dominant definitions of physical beauty. For instance, Martha has liberated hair.[5] She "cuts her hair short, and sometimes it sticks straight up, but she doesn't care" (*Toning*, 18). While peering at her grandmother through a camera lens, Emily thinks: "For the first time in my life I really look at my grandmother. She's beautiful. Her dreads fall over her face when she moves, and her skin glows from sweat" (*Toning*, 32). Similarly, when speaking of her own dreadlocks Ola tells Emily, "I love the way my hair feels. . . . I do wonderful things with it" (*Toning*, 44). Ola considers her hair to be her only vanity; consequently, she refuses chemotherapy in an effort to preserve it. Ola's proclamation concerning the beauty of black hair allows Emily to think positively about her own: "I can't get all of it between my fingers, but I love the way the kinky waves feel" (*Toning*, 45). Emily's experimentation with her hair is a part of her self-discovery. Few cultural critics fail to acknowledge that a large number of black women view hair as an accessory or type of adornment that has a great deal to do with creative expression and self-discovery. Fascinated by styling other's hair, Emily chooses to shave most of hers off but then later considers growing it longer so she can have dreadlocks.

Learning family history, ritual, and tradition are significant in Emily's quest for self-knowledge. David asks, "Do you think about your people, Emmie, your people and their rituals?" (*Toning*, 94). Toward the end of the novel, Emily, with her mother's help, discovers a way to tone the sweep for her grandfather. In the middle of the desert, Emily, clutching a photo of her grandfather, steadies the hammer as her mother takes hold of it. Together they strike a water tower since there is no sweep in the desert. The tower serves their purpose, as the ringing of the metal signals her grandfather to his final resting place and helps her mother bring closure to a painful experience. According to Gregory, toning the sweep "is reminiscent of a West African ritual in which the community comes together and shrieks at the moment of a person's death to strengthen his or her passage between one form of life and another."[6] Together Emily and Diane rediscover a family tradition, one initiated by her grandfather when he and Diane toned the sweep for his own mother. The toning also serves as a reminder that soon they will have to find the strength to tone the sweep for Ola.

Abena P. A. Busia acknowledges, "In this united endeavor to reinterpret our lives in our writings, black women . . . incorporate into their written works some aspect of those . . . arts and folk traditions which have informed their lives."[7] Oftentimes the arts and folk traditions are those derived from Africa. In doing so, black women writers confirm Africa's influence on African American culture. Throughout Johnson's work, there are references to folk culture, storytelling, and the supernatural (e.g., voodoo and ghosts).

Johnson wrote *Toning the Sweep* while spending time with her brother in California. She says, "I just loved the desert. I loved the sunsets." Her brother took her to Little Rock, California, an African American community Johnson believes was developed by people from Little Rock, Arkansas, during the 1950s. Johnson says, "I fell in love with the idea that there was this Little Rock in California. Ultimately, the book came out of loving the desert." Johnson wanted to know how people came to live in Little Rock, so she talked to citizens and was amazed at what she learned. Influenced to write a young adult novel of her own after reading Francesca Lia Block's *Weetzie Bat*, Johnson found the California setting fitting. She recalls, "I loved the idea of [*Toning the Sweep*] being set in California, but very different from *Weetzie Bat*."

The flight motif appears in *Toning the Sweep* and in other novels by Johnson. For example, when *Songs of Faith* begins, the protagonist, Doreen, compares her jump from a building to flight and is disappointed when she believes her father thinks she wants to be a pilot. For Doreen, the thought is limiting. When asked about the recurring references to flight, Johnson says, "My first recurring nightmare as a small child was of a witch kidnapping me and flying me away on her broom. I believe I'm always trying to work it out into a positive." Johnson gives this dream to Marley, the protagonist of *Heaven*.

The flight motif is often found in African American literature, and it manifests itself in several ways. For example, in Toni Morrison's *Song of Solomon* flight refers to the folkloric idea of African slaves who possessed the ability of flight, an ability that freed them as it took them back to their homeland. Lita Hooper refers to the idea of flying from a black feminist perspective. She suggests that African and African American texts often contain female characters confined to "destructive living spaces" who take flight in search of "positive" and "nurturing" environments.[8]

In *Toning the Sweep*, driving becomes a vehicle for flight. When Ola's husband's funeral is over, she takes Diane, packs her husband's Buick, and leaves Alabama, bound for a place where she can raise her daughter free of fear. Ola drives quickly, wildly, and recklessly, instilling fear in others, especially Diane, and then later Emily when she learns that Ola nearly drove her Buick convertible into David. Ola has cherished the car, but in the end it must remain in Little Rock; it must remain in her past. Johnson conveys the importance of letting go of adored people and material possessions. The Buick serves a different purpose for Emily, however. She sneaks out night after night to, she believes, develop driving skills, but in the end the vehicle assists her on her journey to free her grandfather's spirit and her mother's grief, as they tone the sweep together.

Toward the end of the novel, the community comes together to have a party for Ola, who will leave the desert to spend her last days in Ohio battling terminal cancer without the benefit of chemotherapy. During the party, Emily looks through the lens of the camera and captures her grandmother's beauty as she does the fandango. Margaret Title explains, "It's a celebration dance. A dance of life" (*Toning*, 100). Later, Emily says, "I hear Ola laughing. . . . I see her and Martha on a conga line. All the aunts take part" (*Toning*, 100). Ola dances in celebration of her own life and the lives of her progeny. Her dancing suggests that she will continue to live freely, beholden to no one, enjoying the time she has left with her daughter and granddaughter.

Toning the Sweep won Johnson her first, of three, Coretta Scott King Book Awards and was cited as an American Library Association Best Book for Young Adults, a *Booklist* Editors' Choice, and one of the *School Library Journal* Best Books. Barbara Clark, the chair of the Coretta Scott King Book Selection Committee, said about *Toning the Sweep*, "Johnson skillfully captures readers by using letters, soliloquies, and narrative in an emotional family story."[9] Johnson says, "The first time I won the Coretta Scott King [Book] Award, I felt warm all over. The chances of an African American winning a Newbery or Caldecott seems slimmer for some reason. . . . The CSK is in place for us for that wonderful feeling of acclaim."[10]

Critical commentary has focused on the vivid imagery, skillful weaving of past and present events, and accentuation of poetic language that make the book stand out among others and fully engage readers. But critics have also pointed out a few flaws. Betsy Hearne, in a review for the *Bulletin of the Center for Children's Books*, says the novel "runs the risk of being fragmentary."[11] My students agree, complaining that too often Johnson leaves the reader to fill in rather large gaps. The novel, like most of Johnson's fiction, has very little action; it is the relationships between mothers and daughters, the uncovering of family secrets, and Ola's pending demise that compel readers to complete the thin novel.

HEAVEN (1998)

Johnson's treatment of family stresses its importance, strength, and sustenance. Her picture books mark the beginnings of her conscious effort to explore familial relationships. For example, *Daddy Calls Me Man* includes a young male protagonist who watches in awe as his parents create art in their home.[12] In four poems, Johnson describes how the boy interacts with his family and learns to help his parents take care of his little sister. The picture book stresses the importance of family members, regardless of age, working together to contribute to the success of the family unit.[13] Similarly, *When I Am Old with You* emphasizes the significance of intergenerational relationships within families. In her first two novels, *Toning the Sweep* and *Humming Whispers*, Johnson includes family structures that differ from the nuclear family. These families contain foster parents and children and members of the extended family who take on the sole responsibility of raising children they did not give birth to. Thus, family becomes an expansive term including othermothers and people who may not be biologically related. This focus on family is explored more fully in *Heaven* than in any of her other novels, as Johnson maintains that there are multiple ways of defining family and how it influences one's identity development.

As *Heaven* opens, Marley is taking the 1,637 steps from her home to the Western Union inside Ma's Superette to wire money to Uncle Jack (*Heaven*, 6). Though Marley has been wiring money to Jack since she was very young, she realizes she does not know much about him. She has only seen pictures of him as a boy standing alongside her father, Jack's twin brother, and their dog, Boy. Marley's family seems to be a typical working-class family that, long after her mother found the postcard postmarked Heaven, Ohio, and became determined to settle there, has managed to become a part of the community. Though it is June, Johnson skillfully flashes back to the past as Marley recalls meeting her best friend, Shoogy, applying to babysit Bobby Morris's daughter, Feather, and reading letters written by Jack. The blend of past and present is so tightly woven that only a careful read can detect the slippage of time.

In one scene, Marley and her friends take a trip to the country, yet a letter from Jack dated May 24th refers to pictures of Marley and her friends in a similar setting obviously taken during a previous trip (*Heaven*, 29). In another letter, Jack goes to a beach and sees a group of young people similar to the description Johnson offers of Marley and her friends at the beach in the final vignette of part 2, including what Jack refers to as a boy with a baby who was "probably his little sister" (*Heaven*, 84). Interestingly, the letter seems to suggest that Jack is at the same beach along with Marley and her friends, and it is Feather that mesmerizes Boy.

In an interview in *School Library Media Activities Monthly*, Johnson told Carolyn S. Brodie that she gets some of her book ideas from a list of possible book titles that she compiles. "It is really interesting to work this way because the incubus of the entire book is usually the line where the title is actually put in the book. I always find that I can discover an entire world and develop an entire book from just one line or phrase."[14] This seems to be what Johnson accomplished when writing *Heaven*. Not much has "come down in Heaven" (*Heaven*, 36). Yet, Heaven is essential to who Marley believes she is. The place has become a part of her and how she defines herself. Its natural surroundings, especially the river that flows by her home, the buildings, the streets, and of course the people are what have influenced her identity. Thus, Marley's love for her family and community and her comfortableness within them are significant as the novel progresses.

In part 1, Johnson crafts such an idyllic life for Marley that the reader wonders how she will pose problems for her. In part 2, when Marley remembers that Bobby told her that "the Amish trust nature to tell them when a tornado is coming," she resolves, "I now know how to watch for the danger signs" (*Heaven*, 49). In the next section titled "Time," Johnson incorporates a flashback to the day before the storm when the mail carrier, Ethel Grabski, delivered a letter addressed to Mona Floyd. Curious about its contents, Marley dismisses the letter until her parents decide to share it with her. When they do, everything she thought was "true" and "real" isn't. She is not Marley Carroll but Mona Floyd, and her parents are not Lucy and Kevin; they are Christine and Jack.

Christine died in a car accident, and afterward Jack, distraught over his loss, rides around the country with his dog, Boy, gazing at the landscape and observing how people live and interact with one another. Through letters, Johnson reveals Jack's character and foreshadows his return to Marley. Jack's letters are reflective, coded, and filled with a sense of longing for a life he does not have. Each of the letters, two dated several months before the novel actually begins, are written in italics and included in each of the parts except part 2. The letter in part 2 comes from Deacon James David Major in July, and it alters the way Marley perceives herself and notions of family. The tone of Jack's letters change once Deacon Major's letter arrives. They become more formal as he no longer uses affectionate names when he refers to her. Instead, he pleads with her and patiently waits for her anger to dissipate.

Marley spends the remainder of the novel trying to regain her identity, trying to rediscover herself and the people she believed were her biological family. She looks to her friends and the people in the community and finds multiple types of family. The families in the small town of Heaven, Ohio, seem to be working class, but the Maples differ. The Maples are middle class; they indulge in luxuries not available to the other families. For example, Shoogy's parents encourage her to compete in beauty pageants while they play tennis, drive a luxury car, and hire landscape artists to manicure their lawn.

Shoogy Maples's family seems perfect, but Marley realizes that there are flaws. Marley says, "Shoogy told me when I first met her that she used to cut herself so it would block out pain. . . . She told me that she couldn't cut deep enough" (*Heaven*, 93). It is clear to Marley that Shoogy finds it difficult being a member of a family like the Maples, but she is surprised when she discovers that despite Shoogy's criticism of her family, she loves them and longs to be accepted by them.

Bobby Morris's family provides Marley with yet another example. Bobby is raising his daughter, Feather, alone, yet his small family does not seem to contain less love. Johnson reveals Bobby's warmth through how he expresses his love for Feather. He is protective of his daughter (*Heaven*, 34), and he often "looks at Feather as if she is the only baby in the whole world" (*Heaven*, 26). Ma, the owner of the Superette, though childless, offers Marley another glimpse at a nontraditional family structure. Ma's nephew, Chuck, has become a son to her. Marley remarks, "Chuck was better than a son to Ma, and he wasn't her blood son" (*Heaven*, 77). After examining the different types of family around her, Marley begins to understand that family is "the people who have always been there for you" (*Heaven*, 99).

As critics have pointed out, the novel raises several minor questions: Why did Marley's adoptive parents change her name and their last names? Is Jack staying in Heaven long before he writes the final letter announcing his return? Has Jack written to Marley and told her the story about being taken to the beach by her biological parents, or does she remember it? If Jack did not tell her the story, why is the font different, and why is it written in Jack's voice? These questions do not subtract from the novel's appeal. The structure of *Heaven* is reminiscent of the structure of *The First Part Last*. It has four parts, each divided by gray, shadowy double-page spreads that convey the significance of storms, both real and metaphoric, in the characters' lives. Toward the end of the novel Jack tells Marley that her biological mother, Christine, decided to face her fear, and any fear she might have passed on to Marley, of storms by sitting in a porch swing singing to her newborn baby as she "faced the storm down" (*Heaven*, 138). It is this memory that Marley grasps as the novel ends.

Heaven is an exceptional novel because of Johnson's ability to warrant emotional involvement from the reader. Marley's experience resonates with readers, even those who have not been adopted, partly because most of us have wondered or imagined what it would be like to make such a discovery. In a *Booklist* interview Johnson says, "I think a lot of my writing is about the fear and the discovery of the big lie. There's always that point when kids rifle through their parents' papers to make sure they weren't adopted. I was probably about nine or ten when I picked my dad's lockbox with a bobby pin. And it's really interesting because I didn't have that big lie in my life! But I had so many friends who did."[15] Another thing that makes the novel powerful is Johnson's skill in capturing the essence of how one might respond after discovering that they are not who they thought they were. Marley's brother, Butchy, searches through his parents' things, curious about his own parentage, while Marley experiences an array of realistic emotions from anger to depression. Feeling betrayed, she sleeps late in an effort to avoid her parents, and she wonders if she can ever trust them again.

Heaven won the thirtieth annual Coretta Scott King Book Award and a place on the American Library Association Best Books list. When asked about the necessity of the award, Johnson says, "The CSK is a wonderful acknowledgement for African American authors and illustrators, and there is still an incredible need for it. Of course, in a perfect world there would be no need for any awards. We'd all be appreciated and loved for our individual talents, black, white." The focus of the next chapter is on those books that illustrate Johnson's talent for creating circumstances that change those characters who feel they already have some sense of self. Devastated, Johnson's characters are down but never completely out. They accept new challenges and create ways to make difficult situations palatable. They problem solve, a skill Johnson believes is important for young people to develop.

NOTES

1. This chapter is adapted from the author's unpublished doctoral dissertation, KaaVonia Hinton-Johnson, "Expanding the Power of Literature: African American Literary Theory and Young Adult Literature" (Ph.D. diss., The Ohio State University, 2003).

2. Angela Johnson, *Heaven* (New York: Simon & Schuster Books for Young Readers, 1998), 110.

3. Mary Helen Washington, ed., *Invented Lives: Narratives of Black Women 1860–1960* (Garden City, N.Y.: Anchor Press Doubleday & Company, Inc., 1987), xxi.

4. Lorraine Bethel, "This Infinity of Conscious Pain: Zora Neale Hurston and the Black Female Literary Tradition," in *All the Women Are White, All the Blacks Are Men, But Some of Us Are Brave: Black Women's Studies*, eds. Gloria T. Hull, Patricia Bell Scott, and Barbara Smith (New York: The Feminist Press, 1982), 186.

5. Alice Walker, "Oppressed Hair Puts a Ceiling on the Brain," *Ms.* (June 1988), 52–53.

6. Lucille H. Gregory, "Angela Johnson," in *Twentieth-Century Children's Writers*, 4th ed., ed. L. S. Berger (Detroit: St. James Press, 1995), 493–94.

7. Abena P. A. Busia, "Words Whispered over Voids: A Context for Black Women's Rebellious Voices in the Novel of the African Diaspora," in *Studies in Black American Literature Volume III: Black Feminist Criticism and Critical Theory*, eds. Joseph Weixlmann and Houston A. Baker, Jr. (Greenwood, Fla.: The Penkeville Publishing Company, 1988), 14.

8. Lita Hooper, "A Black Feminist Critique of *The Bride Price* and *The Bluest Eye*," *Journal of African Children's and Youth Literature* 6 (1994/1995), 75.

9. Pamela Goodes and Pamela Wallace, "Top Books for Children," *About . . . Time* 22, no. 3 (March 31, 1994), 32.

10. Retrieved from http://www.virginiahamilton.com/pages/looking_for _america.htm on 18 March 2005.

11. Betsy Hearne, "Review of Toning the Sweep," *Bulletin of the Center for Children's Books* 46, no. 10 (June 1993), 318.

12. Angela Johnson, *Daddy Calls Me Man* (New York: Orchard, 1997), unpaginated (hereafter cited as *DCMM*).

13. KaaVonia Hinton, "Affirming African American Boys," *Booklist* (January, 2005), 63.

14. Carolyn S. Brodie, "A Conversation with an Award-Winning Author," *School Library Activities Monthly* 17, no. 10 (June 2001), 44.

15. Gillian Engberg, "The Booklist Interview: Angela Johnson," *Booklist* 100, no. 12 (February 15, 2004), 1,074.

Chapter Five

Discovering Change

"Everything has changed around here, and it just can't be like it was," insists thirteen-year-old Doreen, the protagonist of *Songs of Faith*, one of Johnson's earlier novels.[1] Several books that followed, including the award-winning *The First Part Last*, and the author's latest, *Bird*, feature characters who share Doreen's sentiment. Often family members whom they love and trust cause these changes, while at other times it is the young adult who makes the decision that changes his or her life forever. Johnson says that each of her characters are her "shadows," faint traces of parts of her. Her characters are constantly being challenged by life experiences.

SONGS OF FAITH (1998)

It is 1975, and the small town of Harvey, Ohio, is preparing to celebrate the bicentennial. Thirteen-year-old Doreen and her family live just outside of the projects, physically as well as financially. As Doreen spray paints yellow smiling faces on the bicentennial signs near the projects, she wonders what there is to celebrate. Changes in the town's economic condition suggest that the projects might expand. The pawn shops have been "doing pretty good since the mills have started closing," and the population seems to be made up of working-class single mothers and their children (*Faith*, 1). In addition to this, the town reeks of pollution, suggesting its inhabitants' despair. Families that can afford to are moving away, but some of Harvey's citizens continue to remain, hoping conditions will improve. The bleak setting is linked to Doreen's struggle to patiently wait for better times. Her parents' divorce is final, and everyone responds to it differently. Mama Dot, a factory worker, attends college with hopes of securing a position as an art curator, a job she believes will keep them out of the projects, and Doreen's brother, affectionately called Bobo, becomes Robert and refuses to speak.

When Doreen thinks of her younger brother's attributes, she pales in comparison. It is Robert who is attractive, charming, confident, likeable, goal oriented, and intelligent, while she sees herself as average. After only a few chapters, it becomes clear that she has underestimated herself. It is Doreen who manages to quickly adapt and keep the family together in her father's absence. She becomes the protector, watching after her brother and her mother, who is so consumed with studying that she ignores her children. With no one to turn to, Doreen discovers her inner strength and manages to cope on her own terms with her parents' divorce and the additional responsibilities placed on her by Mama Dot. Doreen also finds comfort from an unlikely source, her neighbor Jolette Thomas. When Doreen meets Jolette, she believes she and Robert are well adjusted to their father's absence; but she soon learns otherwise.

Doreen makes it clear that she would not normally befriend Jolette because Jolette is two years younger, too skinny, and virtually friendless. Doreen becomes even more skeptical of her when Doreen's best friend, Viola, reports that she saw Jolette kill a dog. Doreen and Viola immediately decide Jolette's behavior is strange, but Mama Dot insists that Jolette is different and that "Different isn't good or bad, . . . just different" (*Faith*, 7). Soon Doreen realizes that Robert and Jolette have become friends, so she decides to protect Robert by spending time with them. In the interim, Doreen learns more about Jolette and finds that their circumstances are similar. Jolette becomes a foil for Doreen, suggesting to Doreen that she will eventually begin to heal and make sense of what has happened to her family. Jeff Miller helps Jolette accomplish this, and it is suggested that Jolette will assist Doreen in a similar way.

Jolette's insight goes well beyond her eleven years. Being both abandoned and then moved from place to place affords her a certain awareness that Doreen, though she is two years older, has not grasped. When Doreen suggests that Jolette's new home has been abandoned for years and is probably inhabited by ghosts, Jolette simply replies, "There's worse things in life to worry about" (*Faith*, 6). Yet, after such a profound statement, Johnson is careful to indicate that Jolette is still a child, as Jolette does not answer Doreen when she asks her to explain what she means. Instead, Jolette tries to engage Robert in a game of tag, hitting him and running out of the yard.

Later, Doreen learns that Jolette's father fought in the Vietnam War. The war has also affected Doreen's family. Doreen has not seen her uncle, Mama Dot's brother, in six years because he fled to Canada after refusing to fight. The family stopped watching television completely when one of Mama Dot's friends in high school died in the war (*Faith*, 32). These experiences help Doreen understand that the war is not a television sitcom as she previously thought; but when Jolette reveals how her father was affected by fighting in it, she is certain that the war changed lives in dreadful ways. Jolette's father is like the speaker's father in *The Other Side: Shorter Poems*. He also screams and cries after dreaming about combat in Vietnam. "I didn't know it," the speaker confides, "but that war in the jungle / had followed my daddy all the way to Shorter" (*Other Side*, 39).

It is suggested that Jolette's father, haunted by what he experienced while serving in the military, abandoned her after years of exhibiting unstable behavior. While Jolette's stepmother, Miss Mary, turned to religion to help her cope with her husband's actions, Jolette told herself that the father she once knew would return to her if she jumped rope one million times (*Faith*, 96). Though Jolette's father never resurfaces, Jeff Miller, named after someone Johnson attended high school with, does.

As in other novels by Johnson, Doreen lives in a community where men come for only a brief stay. But when they arrive, they are sensitive, caring, and thoughtful. Johnson positions Jeff as an angelic figure "with an Afro" wandering about the United States caring for the families of men in his platoon who served in the Vietnam War (*Faith*, 67). He follows Doreen and her friends around for a while before telling them who he is and why he has come. Though he intends to help Jolette, what he finds is a "lotta kids running 'round Harvey needing guardian angels" (*Faith*, 67). In the end, Jeff helps them all see their circumstances differently, including Mama Dot.

A reviewer for *Publisher's Weekly* maintains, "Although [Johnson's] sparse novel gives only a sketchy depiction of the heroine's father, readers will feel the impact of his absence on his children and wife."[2] Readers also notice the love and concern he has for his children. After several failed attempts to get Robert to speak to him, he travels to Harvey to see Robert and Doreen. While he is there, it is decided that he will take care of Robert until he is better, while Doreen will remain in Harvey with Mama Dot. Influenced by Jolette, Robert told himself that if he stopped speaking, his father would return home. Unexpectedly, his father does not remain with the family. Instead, Robert is separated from his mother and sister. This is yet another change Doreen must navigate.

As Johnson often does, she uses weather imagery to foreshadow upcoming events that adversely change characters' lives.[3] In *Heaven*, for example, a turbulent storm comes just before Marley learns she is adopted. Similarly, in the blazing summer heat, Doreen realizes her parents' divorce is final; when the leaves begin to fall, Robert stops speaking completely, and when it snows, Doreen feels her life is barren because her father leaves a second time and takes her brother to live in Chicago with him. Doreen realizes she has to be strong as she tries to steady herself in the midst of constant movement, as Robert's departure comes soon after her best friend Viola moves to New Haven, Connecticut, and Jeff Miller moves on to help another needy family.

The novel's end is somber though Johnson suggests that Doreen is hopeful. Jolette has made snow angels all around Doreen's yard, and her mother is redecorating with the paint she used to alter the bicentennial signs, suggesting providence and renewal. Johnson makes it clear that Doreen has matured and developed in ways that allow her to persevere. *Songs of Faith* is based on Johnson's experiences as an adolescent and an adult. Deeply reminiscent of Johnson's feelings of both separation from and emergence into the adult world while still in her teens, she says, "[The book] seems so personal to me now." Johnson says it was written during a time when she was still uncertain about the direction she wanted to take as a writer. Faced with change in her writing career, including feeling divorced from aspects of the publishing world, she was "between editors and publishing houses."

Though a *Booklist* reviewer of *Songs of Faith* writes, "As in *Toning the Sweep* (1993), Johnson shows the misunderstandings and powerful love in families and offers a fascinating group of characters to illustrate her theme: the permanence of love in a world that is always changing," the book, eclipsed by the Coretta Scott King Book Award winner, *Heaven*, was largely overlooked by critics.[4] However, others who reviewed the book called it heart wrenching, eloquent, and tender.

BIRD (2004)

In Johnson's most recent novel, *Bird*, the title character must adapt when her stepfather, Cecil, decides he no longer wants to be a part of her family. Having lost a father before, she has no intention of losing another one. At thirteen years old, Bird leaves Cleveland, Ohio, traveling south to Acorn, Alabama, where she hopes to find Cecil and convince him to return home with her. When the novel begins, there is a storm indicating that Bird is in the midst of a difficult situation. Wet, cold, and sitting in a small shed, Bird says, "All I could think about was when I'd be dry again. I didn't think I ever would be."[5] To Bird, the storm is a metaphor for turmoil, while dryness signifies happiness. Several times Bird says, "Never have seen this much rain in my whole life" (*Bird*, 2). Bird has been hiding in a shed in the woods for three weeks waiting for opportunities to frequent the home of Cecil's relatives undetected. She is successful until Ethan, unable to conceal his interest in her any longer, decides to come forth, introduce himself, and openly help her by providing food and interesting conversation. Bird knows who Ethan is since she has seen him in Cecil's family photos, photos of people he refuses to share with Bird and her mother.

Ethan's delicate health and recent heart transplant have kept him from children his own age and denied him the opportunity to bond with youth outside his family until he meets Bird. When Bird leaves, he is heartbroken but distracts himself by spending time with his Uncle C. L., Bird's stepfather. In this novel, Johnson introduces a different type of family dynamic: two types of family connected, yet disconnected, by one individual. This connection is not revealed until Cecil arrives at Ethan's home and is only a few feet away from where Bird is hiding.

Not sure where she will go next, Bird meets fourteen-year-old Jay as he pines the loss of his brother, an organ donor, and his recent house-arrest sentence for plotting with his best friend, Googy, to take elderly Mrs. Pritchard's truck for a joyride. According to Johnson, Googy is Shoogy of *Heaven*'s cousin, two characters who will be fully developed

in Johnson's tentatively titled *Sweet*, a companion novel to *Heaven* and
The First Part Last.

In alternating chapters, the voices of Bird, Ethan, and Jay tell inter-
twining stories about change, love, loss, forgiveness, and reconciliation.
The main characters in *Bird* are connected to each other and to Mrs.
Pritchard though they really do not know each other. Interestingly, the
two families distance themselves from each other though Ethan and his
mother plant rose bushes in Jay's yard. Jay knows Ethan has his brother
Derek's heart and wonders if Derek's thoughts and interests will now
live on in Ethan. It is Bird, a geographical outsider, who illuminates the
connection, though Ethan and Jay realize it exists. Johnson says she believes in the circle of life. "We are all connected," she says.

In a *Booklist* review of *Bird*, Gillian Engberg writes, "Some of the
connections between characters seem stretched." But she goes on to
commend the author, claiming, "Johnson writes with a poet's knowledge
of rhythm and knows how to use the space between words."[6] In the end,
all three characters find some comfort and a new way to survive in the
midst of pain, disappointment, and fear of things unknown. Ethan, no
longer afraid that his heart will stop working, runs, swims, and tries
other forms of physical activity. He decides to relish his second chance
at life by attending school for the first time and forming friendships. Jay
apologizes to Mrs. Pritchard and simultaneously forgives himself for
being cruel to his brother, especially the morning of the day he died of
a brain aneurysm.

Johnson has given Jay her passion for books, as he finds solace in
them. She once described her parents' negative reaction when she and
her brothers sat at the dinner table reading. But Jay's parents, steeped in
grief, do not seem to notice. Also, with Mrs. Pritchard's help, Bird realizes it is time to go home to her mother and forget about a stepfather
who could so easily desert her. It takes time and a growing sense of maturity before Bird begins to see Cecil's character clearly. Up until the
end of the novel, Bird hopes she will discover how Ethan's family manages to keep Cecil happy so that she and her mother can change to make
themselves more appealing to him. Cecil is one of only a few of Johnson's male characters who seem to disregard those who love them.
When Bird has the opportunity to confront Cecil, she refuses, conclud-
ing that he is, as Johnson describes him, "totally removed."

Cecil is a runner. When he invites Bird on his early morning runs, he
tells her she "has the energy of a hummingbird" (*Bird*, 9). Aside from

this one, most of Bird's memories of Cecil suggest he is self-absorbed, distant, and unkind. While observing from a distance, she learns he has two identities. Bird and her mother never really come to know the loving Uncle C. L. Ethan adores. Cecil's brief visits to Alabama illustrate his inability to give of himself for extended periods of time. Ethan recalls that Cecil began running in order to escape the physical abuse he was subjected to as a child and concludes, "Uncle C. L. will always be running away from something" (*Bird*, 49). Soon Bird realizes that she is a runner too, another person who leaves those who love them behind. Memories of her mother reveal a loving mother-daughter relationship, one she realizes she needs to get back to if she hopes to put an end to the loneliness she feels. Johnson says Cecil's character is loosely based on someone she knew who lived with a significant other for years without really knowing very much about him.

The geographical location of this novel is especially significant to Johnson. When she begins to speak about *Bird* she says, "*Bird* is Alabama, the red dirt, the ponds; that's definitely Alabama. Actually, I based it on a little enclave in Shorter." When Johnson was born in a hospital on the campus of Tuskegee University, her parents took her home with them to Shorter, where the family lived for a while and still visits. In *Bird*, there are references to the greyhound racetrack that Johnson mentions in *The Other Side*.

In this novel and in her other work Johnson expresses the importance of self-actualization, of discovering ways inside oneself to cope with change and the loss that is often associated with it. Johnson wrote *The First Part Last* and *Bird* while working through a tragic change in her own life. She says, "I lost a friend, and I was really throwing myself into my work; so I wrote these books [*A Cool Moonlight*, *The First Part Last*, and *Bird*], all of them at one time." It was also during a time when our nation was facing what would become a change in the way we perceived the country's vulnerability, as terrorists destroyed the World Trade Center.

THE FIRST PART LAST (2003)

In *The First Part Last*, Bobby, the single father who first appeared in *Heaven*, describes the events that led to his daughter Feather's birth, his girlfriend Nia's illness, and his decision to take on the responsibility of raising his daughter.[7] The novel is divided into four parts and told in alternate chapters headed "now" and "then." As Johnson writes, she tends to create nonlinear vignettes with little regard to time sequence or extensive description. She says, "To me, there are no boundaries with time." Kevin Lewis, her editor, noticed a particular pattern developing as she wrote *The First Part Last* and suggested the "now" and "then" structure.

The beautiful cover of a young man supposedly holding his newborn child—he is actually holding his own niece—conveys both the strength and vulnerability Bobby expresses throughout the novel. When discussing the cover, Johnson says, "Look at how much power this tiny little baby has over him. It would have been wrong if he had been smiling. It's so intense; he has to be blown away. [His facial expression suggests] 'This kid is going to change my entire life.' Which they do." Echoing Johnson, Bobby says, "Things have to change. I've been thinking about it. Everything. And when Feather opens her eyes and looks up at me, I already know there's change."[8]

When the book begins, Feather is only a few days old, and Bobby is reflecting on his childhood and how it connects to his new understandings of parenthood. Bobby acknowledges that having unprotected sex with his girlfriend, Nia, despite their knowledge of the importance of safe sex and the accessibility of condoms made available by Bobby's mother, was irresponsible. But he also admits that this did not become clear to him until his sixteenth birthday, when he arrives home to find Nia on his doorstep offering him a balloon along with the news that she is pregnant. Together, they must consider if they will allow the pregnancy to impact their lives or terminate it. Bobby is an intelligent young man, scheduled to graduate from high school at sixteen, and Nia is also bright and ambitious. But since there is now a baby to consider, college is no longer a possibility. As time progresses, the number of options available to the couple are reduced to one: adoption. This too will further change their lives, as neither of them is comfortable raising a child or giving one up to be raised by someone else so that they can "get on with it [the future]" (*First Part*, 97). The couple finally decides, with slight pressure from their parents, to put the baby up for adoption. Bobby never seems comfortable with this decision, so it is not surprising when he decides to keep Feather himself when Nia descends into a vegetative state due to eclampsia.

Bobby's decision to take care of Feather is his attempt to prove his manhood to Just Frank and to himself. But being a man is not easy, and throughout the novel he sits at the border, not quite a man but too experienced to be a boy. Bobby realizes that Feather is not a doll, to be held and admired, when she gets sick and he has to take her to the hospital. Helpless and inept, he sits alone waiting for Feather to recover. "This must be it. The place where you really feel that it's all on you and you got a kid" (*First Part*, 32). In part 2, Bobby decides to become a carefree and careless teen again when he leaves Feather with his neighbor, Coco, vandalizes city property, and is arrested. Prior to this incident, he constantly thinks of abandoning fatherhood altogether and of begging his parents for more help. Bobby surrenders to the irresponsible desires he has harbored all along, and it is at this point that Bobby realizes that he will not be able to live in New York much longer. In the first section of part 3, Bobby describes himself inside a fairy-tale world where his existence is anything but extraordinary. He simply longs to be a sixteen-year-old having fun with his friends, free of the adult responsibility of taking care of an infant.

In part 4, Bobby moves to Brooklyn where he will receive more support and supervision from his father. He will also be closer to Feather's babysitter, so he will no longer have to wake up several hours earlier to take Feather to the babysitter before going to school. A visit from his brother Paul encourages him to consider raising Feather in Heaven, Ohio. Critics wrongly suggest Johnson does not explain Bobby's reasons for leaving New York, the city he loves, and the support of his parents. However, Bobby's motive is clearly revealed. His nightmares involve his being apprehended by police, showing that he realizes New York is ripe with opportunities to find more trouble for himself. Bobby says, "The city just feels like it's too big," and like most parents he wonders if a large city is an appropriate place for rearing his daughter (*First Part*, 128). Above all, Bobby realizes that with his parents and kind neighbors like Coco being in New York increases his chances of shirking his responsibility and leaving Feather to others to raise.

Shortly after *The First Part Last* was awarded the 2004 Michael L. Printz and Coretta Scott King awards, Johnson told *Booklist* the novel was "the last book . . . [she] thought would ever get this much attention."[9] Darwin Henderson, a member of the International Reading Association committee that chose the 2004 Michael L. Printz award winners, says the book stood out because of "the writing style and emotional depth."[10] Johnson says that she thanks her editor and a group of sixth-grade girls at the Manhattan School for Children who were enamored of Bobby in the prequel, *Heaven*, for suggesting that she write the book. While in New York, she says she saw a young man on the subway who inspired her further. In her acceptance speech for the Printz award Johnson comments, "As I never intended to write *The First Part Last*, I had to come to understand that sometimes the muse is not always in control but that others' visions are sometimes stronger, clearer than your own."[11]

A reviewer in *Publisher's Weekly* said, "The only misstep [in *The First Part Last*] is a chapter from Nia's point of view, which takes readers out of Bobby's capable hands."[12] As in *Toning the Sweep*, where sections of the book are printed in italics and express the thoughts and feelings of David Two Starr, Diane, and Ola, in part 4 Nia offers her childhood hopes and dreams as she drifts into a coma awaiting flight.

Johnson challenges socially constructed notions of race and gender, depicting black males who are both masculine and nurturing, as are Bobby, his father, and his brother, while the females are firm and no-nonsense but also loving. Bobby's race is significant, as he is a black teen committing to raising a child while black males are often portrayed as negligent and unconcerned. Johnson says, "I love Bobby. I love the idea of a Bobby. I get sick of everybody seeing young black males as irresponsible." Similarly, it is no accident that in *Songs of Faith*, Doreen's brother Robert becomes mute instead of Doreen. It is also Robert who cries freely while Doreen holds back; but when her father reminds her for the final time that things have changed between him and Mama Dot, she gives in: "I can't help it. I cry."

Johnson told Todd R. Nelson, "I was surrounded by very nurturing men. My mother worked second shift when we were little kids, and my father made dinner, took us shopping, carted us around. My brother is the same way with his little daughter. Bobby came from being around these very nurturing males."[13] Because of Johnson's concern for how males are often portrayed in media, she was drawn to creating a character similar to men she knows and loves, like her father and brothers.

But Johnson also suggests that Bobby's character itself had a great deal to do with how he is depicted. In her Printz acceptance speech she describes Bobby's dialogue: "Think about what I'm doing here with this baby," he said. "I'm a young teenage father. The world sees me as just another black boy who's got a baby. I want to be a man, a father. I'm growing up before your eyes if you let me."[14]

Johnson was astounded when an interviewer expressed shock at learning that Bobby is black. Johnson describes her dealings with race as simplistic but argues that the cover of her book indicates that the protagonist is black. Johnson says, "Now, I found it really interesting that this woman didn't look at the young man on the cover with dreadlocks and see him as African American. I just take it for granted that all of my main characters are African American." In a review of *Songs of Faith*, Kathleen Isaacs writes, "Once again Johnson has set attractive and realistic African American characters in situations in which race is not the focus."[15] Johnson is not overt about Bird's race either, and the cover of a shadowy image of a girl's lower body perched on a tree limb does not reveal much, though dirt "makes her skin look rusty brown and dry" (*Bird*, 35).

She chooses to focus directly on issues of importance to her characters, and race is usually not significant to them. The only book thus far that Johnson admits to being deliberately ambiguous about the character's race is *A Cool Moonlight*, the story of eight-year-old Lila who has xeroderma pigmentosum, which makes her sensitive to light. Johnson says she got the idea to write the story after reading a magazine article, but she decided—while lying on what she refers to as a "beautiful tropical sort of paradise" in Aruba—that Lila did not need a race. Johnson explains, "There were all kinds of wonderful people on the beach. There were African American, Spanish, and Norwegian people, people from all over the planet. Incredibly beautiful people, and they were all together. There was no separation." Johnson says that at that moment she began to wonder what life would be like if we all lived in the dark. What would happen if our interactions with people were not influenced by physical appearance but by "the timber of their voice, their soul?" Johnson continues, "I thought Lila would be this child who lives in this world. It was very important to me that if I ever got to write, brown faces and caramel faces and dark chocolate faces would be in the pages of my books. But Lila sort of took on a world that I really didn't have any control of, so she is what she is."

Johnson's lack of representation of race and racial issues raises several questions: Does Johnson feel she must exclude racial issues in order to reach a mainstream audience, or does she merely deal with themes that are universal in an effort to convey the human nature found in us all? One of the important aspects of Johnson's books is the wide range of African American experience they convey. Often critics make note of Johnson's universal themes as if they are out of place in a novel by and about African Americans. The most powerful thing her work does is challenge reader's thinking about what African American children's literature is and whom it is for. Despite this, another question must still be posed: does her work suggest that racism is no longer a concern for blacks, particularly the black middle class, and, if so, isn't this problematic?

While *Toning the Sweep* vaguely deals with a racial issue, it is set in the past as if that's where racism exists. In *Heaven*, Johnson indirectly addresses the racially motivated church burnings instead of taking the issue on. One of the few places where Johnson tackles racial discrimination is in a short poem in *Running Back to Ludie* titled "Boulders." Within the poem, the speaker wishes for a boulder that will force people to "brush up against / people they don't like because of / their cars, what they eat and / the / color / of their skin" (*Ludie*, 9).

Some readers question Johnson's failure to ascribe racial identities to minor characters. When describing the discussion of ethnicity in *Toning the Sweep* during a mother-daughter book group meeting, Susan R. Farber claims, "the main characters are African American, but, interestingly, the author never states the race of their friends."[16] For example, Johnson does not address the racial identities of Ms. Sally Hirt, Roland, or some of the others. Similarly, the racial identities of most of the characters are obscure in *Gone from Home*, *Looking for Red*, and *The First Part Last*. Though Johnson includes biracial characters in both, it is obvious in only one of the novels. In *Looking for Red*, Mark boasts about being black Irish: his mother is Irish, and his father is black. When talking about race in *The First Part Last*, Johnson says Nia is also biracial.

Johnson says that today's young adults are faced with problems that seemed far removed from her own generation. She recalls, "When I graduated from high school, I knew one person under the age of eighteen who had a baby, and she was married. That was just a little over twenty years ago." Johnson believes adults minimize or fail to acknowledge the extent to which this particular societal change impacts young people. Johnson says, "I just take it for granted that if you truly love kids you look at their lives realistically." She recalls a parent she met at a recent book signing who told her she did not want her daughter to read *The First Part Last* because she "didn't want to give her any ideas." Johnson says, "I'm thinking 'give her any ideas'? When did it get to the point where you have to give teenagers ideas about having sex? That's just a little unrealistic, isn't it?"

Some of my students have similar views. They wonder if the book, in the hands of impressionable adolescents, might send a message that glorifies teen pregnancy. They fear that young girls might look past Nia's fate and only see that Bobby loves Nia and the baby enough to take care of Feather. Some of the prospective teachers in my classes fear that adolescent girls might hope their boyfriends will do the same, especially those who yearn to have someone to love. Further, they claim the book could possibly encourage adolescent girls to commit to beginning a family when they are obviously not ready for such a responsibility.

One of Johnson's colleagues told her about a young man whom Johnson says "hated *The First Part Last*." He had trouble accepting a story about a young man who is actually happy about having a baby. Recalling the boy's response Johnson says, "His take on it was [that Bobby] should have been miserable and he shouldn't have done it." The "it" Bobby shouldn't have done is committing to raising Feather. Johnson continues, "You have to wonder what's happened in this kid's life." Recalling the young man's statement Johnson says emphatically, "Bobby wasn't this free-spirited happy kid. His girlfriend is in a coma. [After he made the decision to keep Feather,] his mother said, 'You're going to be a daddy. You're not going to hand this child off.' His father said, 'I love you, but *you're* going to do it.'"

For some novice critics this does not seem to be enough adversity. My students argued that the portrayal is unrealistic—many of the females find it difficult to accept that a young man would take on such a responsibility. Conversely, one of the male students in the class found the book to be realistic and could name several close acquaintances who had taken on the responsibility of raising children. Critics seem to agree with Johnson. They argue that the book "shows [teens] how hard it is to raise a baby."[17] Reviewer Neal A. Lester sums it up: the book is "a cautionary tale . . . [it] is . . . a litany of how past mistakes forever haunt these young characters' present dreams and future realities."[18]

But Lester waivers when he writes, "Although Johnson's story is a valiant effort to bring us a perspective not often considered—that of a young single father fully embracing his new role—the story seems at odds with itself."[19] According to Lester, Bobby and Nia act irresponsibly when they continue to have sex after she becomes pregnant. Regardless of criticism concerning Bobby's decisions, Johnson concludes, "In the end, he said that I am this child's father. I am going to screw up, but I'm going to try to get it right."

It is this type of connection and commitment to family that makes Johnson's novels universal. The next chapter explores another universal concern, loss. The devastation and mental stress involved when one loses a family member to illness, abandonment, or death can be overwhelming, but Johnson treats the issue with sensitivity and understanding of her audience's maturity.

NOTES

1. Angela Johnson, *Songs of Faith*. (New York: Orchard, 1998), 20 (hereafter cited as *Faith*).

2. Diane Roback, ed., "Review of *Songs of Faith*," *Publisher's Weekly* 245, no. 2 (January 12, 1998), 60.

3. Kathleen Isaacs, "Review of *Songs of Faith*," *School Library Journal* 44, no. 3 (March 1998), 214.

4. Susan Dove Lempke, "Review of *Songs of Faith*," *Booklist* 94, no. 12 (February 15, 1998), 1,008.

5. Angela Johnson, *Bird* (New York: Dial, 2004), 3.

6. Gillian Engberg, "Review of Bird," *Booklist* 101, no. 1 (September 1, 2004), 108. Academic Search Premier, 29 October 2004. Keyword: Johnson, Angela.

7. Hinton, "Affirming African American Males," 62.

8. Angela Johnson, *The First Part Last* (New York: Simon & Schuster Books for Young Readers.), 4 (hereafter cited as *First Part*).

9. Gillian Engberg, "The Booklist Interview: Angela Johnson," *Booklist* 100, no. 12 (February 15, 2004): 1,074.

10. Anonymous, "The Envelope, Please," *Reading Today* 21, no. 5 (April 1, 2004). Retrieved from http://0-elibrary.bigchalk.com.opac.cadl.org/libweb/elib/do/document on 31 July 2004.

11. Angela Johnson, "The Michael L. Printz Award Speech," *Young Adult Library Services* 3, no. 1 (Fall 2004), 26.

12. Diane Roback, ed., "Review of *The First Part Last*," *Publisher's Weekly* 250, no. 24 (June 16, 2003), 73. Academic Premier. 31 July 2004. Keyword: Johnson, Angela.

13. Todd R. Nelson, "Angela Johnson: Teenage Graceland," *Hope Magazine* (January/February 2004). Retrieved from http://www.hopemag.com/issues/2004/JanFeb/signGraceland.htm on 24 March 2004.

14. Johnson, "The Michael L. Printz Award Speech," 27.

15. Isaacs, "Review of *Songs of Faith*."

16. Susan R. Farber, "Bonding through Books," *School Library Journal* 43, no. 4 (April 1997), 57.

17. Neal A. Lester, "Review of *The First Part Last*," *Journal of Adolescent and Adult Literacy* 47 no. 5 (February 2004), 431. Academic Premier. 31 July 2004.

18. Lester, "Review of *The First Part Last*," 429.

19. Lester, "Review of *The First Part Last*," 430.

Chapter Six

Discovering Loss

"I think it's like walking barefoot in a room full of broken glass when someone you love goes away," says Michaela (Mike), the protagonist of *Looking for Red*.[1] Johnson remembers that "one school denied me speaking privileges because they thought one of the themes in one of my books was a little too much for their children, about a lynching thirty years ago. I write about real life, things universal. I'll never be one to write about puppies and kittens; it's not going to happen."[2] Though the reference refers to school officials' reactions to *Toning the Sweep*, Johnson's comments concerning her interest in writing realistic fiction about daunting topics applies to most of her work, including her second novel, *Humming Whispers*. In *Humming Whispers*, *Running Back to Ludie*, and *Looking for Red* Johnson concentrates on an area that is difficult for most readers, regardless of age, to understand and accept: loss. Each of the books in this chapter features characters who have lost loved ones, either physically or metaphorically.

HUMMING WHISPERS (1995)

Using a friend's apartment in the city of Cleveland as the setting, Johnson begins *Humming Whispers* with a flashback. Sophy's sister Nicole, who is fourteen, hears the humming whispers of the title for the first time and is lured into a busy parking lot. Only four years old, Sophy does not follow when Aunt Shirley leaves the store to search for Nicole.

Sophy marvels at the sights and smells of the store until Aunt Shirley returns. This flashback actually serves to foreshadow the novel's central conflict. While very young, Sophy developed a special bond with Nicole and secretly longs to emulate her, but the bond becomes fragile when Sophy realizes that she might indeed be more like Nicole than she hoped.

Sophy spends a significant amount of time chaperoning her older sibling. In part 1, it becomes clear that Nicole does not make Sophy's responsibility for her easy. She frequently decides not to take the medicine she hides underneath a ceramic Buddha, complaining that it makes her feel like she might "float away" (*Humming*, 70). Tension begins to rise when Nicole turns twenty-five and her boyfriend Rueben and her family meet at her parents' gravesite to celebrate. During the party, Sophy drifts off to sleep to the sound of a fellow mourner playing a bagpipe in the cemetery. When she wakes up, she finds that, once again, Aunt Shirley has left her behind to search for Nicole. This time Nicole is difficult to find. Johnson ends part 1 of the novel with Sophy posting revised signs, indicating Nicole's current age and hairstyle. Johnson plants a much-needed pause into the book, as readers need time to reflect on Nicole's condition and the stress and strain it causes her and those who love her. Readers quickly come to realize that though Aunt Shirley uses words sparingly, they are well chosen and wise: "None of us would get out of this untouched" (*Humming*, 47). This succinct statement is the overarching message of the book, and it stems from Johnson's conversations with numerous people who, unsolicited, told her of their experiences with siblings who have schizophrenia. Johnson says, "I wanted to write about the sadness and hope that everyone [who spoke to her] always lived in for their ill brother or sister."

At the beginning of part 2, Nicole, still in her nightgown, is found at the airport, one of her favorite places to visit. When she is found, the police take her to City Hospital where she must remain for several days. Sophy is determined to help Nicole recover. "Got to make it easy for her to stay out of City this time" (*Humming*, 60). Johnson captures the complexity of the illness by establishing some of the difficulties Nicole faces.

Johnson creates additional tension when Sophy becomes delusional, seeing images of herself in the mirror that are not there. Poverty, prostitution, and despair lurk, suggesting that Sophy has little room to escape adversity. She begins stealing small insignificant things, like cans of lima beans, dishtowels, candy bars, and tubes of lipstick. When Nicole discovers the items in a box under Sophy's bed and questions her about them, Sophy lies to Nicole, unsure of why she is stealing. After Sophy is confronted for shoplifting at Cool Joe Monkey, she takes the boxes of items she has stolen to the street and leaves them there for the neighbors to use.

Frightened and uncomfortable about asking for help, Sophy suffers from the threat of schizophrenia throughout the rest of the novel. In a passage in which Johnson allows Nicole to speak, she reveals that Nicole often follows Sophy around the dangerous neighborhood streets and is aware that Sophy believes she too will become schizophrenic before she turns fifteen. As Nancy Vasilakis points out in *Horn Book Magazine*, Johnson creates such compelling and convincing passages "the reader can never be sure, any more than Sophy is, whether she has inherited the family curse."[3] For instance, Sophy's sanity is really uncertain toward the end of part 2 when she sees a lady dancing. This scene brings about a number of questions: Is the lady real? Is the lady Nicole? Is Sophy dreaming or sleepwalking as she walks to Miss Onyx's house? Johnson does not offer many answers. But by part 3, as Sophy continues to feel her own sanity waning, Nicole seems to slip further away.

Humming Whispers, though different from *Toning the Sweep* in a number of ways, does share some similarities with the debut novel in the portrayal of males, most notably Rueben, who was described by one reviewer as unrealistic. Reuben counters stereotypical images of black males often presented in print and visual media. He is a caregiver, loving and caring for his girlfriend, Nicole, and his mother's longtime friend, Miss Onyx, a Holocaust survivor. Miss Onyx encourages Sophy to hold on to her dream of dancing as she recalls her own youth as a prima ballerina.

Also, the focus on the arts as a significant part of our culture, particularly African American culture, is a recurring focus of Johnson's work. But while Rueben seems to play his saxophone, create ceramic images, and sketch portraits nearly uninhibited by circumstances, the women in the novel do not fare as well. Art cannot save them. They are what Helen Washington terms "thwarted artists," often found in the literature of African American women such as Alice Walker.[4] Unlike Walker's female characters, Johnson's seem thwarted not by racism and sexism but by illness and social class. Aunt Shirley, Nicole and Sophy's guardian, cannot afford to devote time to creating art because she has to work long hours at a tofu factory in order to provide for the family. Sophy studies dance at a performing arts school, as did Nicole. Yet, Nicole's illness and Sophy's fear of becoming mentally ill stunts and limits the development of their talent.

As Hazel Rochman writes in *Booklist*, "Far from a simplistic problem novel, this is a bleak contemporary story of suffering, lit with the hope of people who take care of each other in the storm."[5] Johnson's former editor, Richard Jackson, says she knew a great deal about schizophrenia before deciding to write the novel. Johnson says that when people in her community learned she was writing a book about the illness, they called her, anxious to share their stories with her. However bleak the topic might be, Johnson feels it is important to give voice to those who lose loved ones to mental illness.

RUNNING BACK TO LUDIE (2001)

In an interview with *School Library Media Activities Monthly*, Johnson says that writing novels drains her.[6] Richard Jackson recalls that Johnson was often concerned about the length of her books. He says that while working on *Gone from Home: Short Takes* he told Johnson that the middle of the book needed an additional story—"something sort of light hearted and short." Jackson chuckles as he recalls Johnson's response: "She said, 'Well, short I can do.'" It turned out that Johnson had already done it. Jackson continues, "She looked around at home. She said, 'I found this in a drawer. I don't know. It's crazy.'" Johnson sent a copy of "By the Time You Read This" to Jackson. Of the story, Jackson says, "I thought it was just hilarious, and it's like this spark right in the middle of the book." Johnson's preference for succinct forms of expression stems from her love of writing poetry. She once said she likes the "sense of completion" that writing poetry affords her.[7] Vignettes free her in a similar way.

In an article in *The Horn Book Magazine*, Patty Campbell looks critically at young adult novels in verse, posing important questions such as "Is it poetry?"[8] Campbell concludes that "good verse novels fit that dictionary definition of 'poetry,' especially in their use of condensed language, natural cadences, and metaphor."[9] Campbell continues defining the form, suggesting "that verse novels" are almost always written in the present tense and narrated in the first person by a teen. The text is shaped in a succession of one- or two-page poems, usually titled, that end with a punch line."[10] *Running Back to Ludie* is Johnson's only novel in verse, yet *The Other Side: Shorter Poems* seems to meet Campbell's criteria just as well.

In over thirty poems, *Running Back to Ludie* tells the story of an unnamed adolescent girl whose mother has been absent for most of her life. Raised by her aunt Lucille and her father, the girl often finds comfort in the few memories she has of her mother, Ludie. Those memories seem to provide a superficial connection to Ludie that she desperately needs. Unlike the mother in *The First Part Last* who conveniently goes into an irreversible coma, here Johnson creates a mother who for seemingly no reason decides not to mother her daughter. In a number of the poems, Johnson captures the sense of loss the girl feels. In "Lavender," Ludie sends a lavender-scented letter, asking, "Has it been too long?" as she wants the opportunity to get to know her daughter. The poem ends and then begins again on the opposite page, indicating the length of time the speaker needs to reflect on the content of the letter from Ludie. After the lengthy pause, the speaker answers, "No—not too long . . ." (*Ludie*, 7). And thus begins the speaker's journey to recover loss.

As in her other novels, a depiction of a devoted father is included. When the protagonist wants to visit her mother, her father—who has attended mother-daughter teas, taught her how to drive, and models compassion—is hesitant but supports her decision. Perhaps he senses the inevitable change in their lives that the protagonist only later anticipates. "I get the crazy cold shakes / that something lives / with me, Lucille, and Dad / that won't / leave us like we were" (*Ludie*, 43). When she visits Ludie, she enters a world devoid of any trace of herself. Her mother is no longer called Ludie but Elaine by friends and loved ones she's formed relationships with, "living a life / with people who are / not / me," the speaker laments. In the final poems, Johnson brings about a sense of resolution similar to that found by Pearl in "Home," one of the short stories in *Gone from Home: Short Takes*. The protagonist no longer expects Ludie to be the mother she lost years earlier, but she is happy that Ludie has reentered her life and joins the others on her list of people she loves (*Ludie*, 44).

Interestingly, Johnson's prose seems more poetic than the poetry in *Running Back to Ludie*, and many of the poems, though they reveal authentic adolescent experiences, do not always seem to move the plot forward. "Boulders" and "The Underground Railroad" are examples. In "Boulders," the speaker seems frustrated about race relations in her community. "The Underground Railroad" immediately follows "Boulders," forcing readers to wonder if the protagonist believes that freedom from racism only exists outside the country. Though the story is a compelling one, the poems are largely narrative and lacking in poetic elements. Nina Lindsay, a reviewer for the *School Library Journal*, points out that the poetry pales in comparison to the poems that make up *The Other Side*.[11] Conversely, a *Publisher's Weekly* reviewer states that the poems are "evocative."[12] Nevertheless, the book conveys Johnson's strength as a storyteller, able to pull readers in by providing character details that evoke emotional response. Readers leave *Running Back to Ludie* as they leave all of Johnson's books, caring about what happens to the central characters.

LOOKING FOR RED (2002)

Looking for Red begins with the twelve-year-old protagonist Mike already in the middle of a difficult situation. On the first page, Mike recalls being a beginning reader at four years old, riding on the back of her brother Red's bicycle reading store signs as they speed down the street. The initial flashback describes the close relationship Mike and Red shared and sets the mood for the rest of the novel: a brooding sense of loss, somber reflection, and unconditional love. "Everything was always [Red]," Mike says just before she reveals that he has disappeared (*Red*, 2). As is typical of Johnson's novels, the first vignette raises a number of questions: What happened to Red? Did he run away? Was he abducted? Why does his image appear to her? Is he haunting the coast?

Johnson's vivid images, skillful characterization, and the hint of suspense pull the reader into Mike's community. Suddenly, it becomes clear that *Looking for Red* is a type of mystery novel. Johnson offers her first clue, actually a red herring, indicating Red's demise when Mike recalls a storm that left her concerned for Red's safety. Throughout the novel, along with Mike, Red's friends Mark and Mona express an odd mixture of grief and guilt. Readers don't learn why until the end of the book when Johnson reveals how Red died.

The novel's momentum increases when Mark runs his 1965 Mustang into Nemo's Fresh Seafood store. Though the adults think he tried to kill himself to join his best friend, Mona and Mike know Mark is seeking redemption. Mark hopes that destroying the car and writing a letter to Red will settle the debt he owes. It's been three months since Red's death, and he seems to haunt them. Mona sits in front of Red's house waiting for him week after week, until, finally unable to bear the loss any longer, she leaves town. The appearance and then reappearance of at least two ghosts suggests that the novel might have been influenced by Virginia Hamilton's *Sweet Whispers, Brother Rush*. Oddly, in order to establish a history of ghosts haunting the cape, Mike recalls that her grandfather, also called Red, appeared as a ghost and protected her and Red when they ran away to live on the beach at the ages of six and nine. Though this is a strange addition to the plot, it illustrates the surreal connection Red seemed to have with his grandfather and with Mike. "But all this is just to let you know. They've been hanging around here for a long time. The ghosts. So it isn't so unbelievable that they're around us now" (*Red*, 80).

Johnson's environmentalist and animal-rights concerns, themes that are also included in some of her short stories, surface. The subplot centers on neighbor and family friend Jo's concern for commercial developers moving onto beach property. Initially, it is suggested that she sabotaged the workers' equipment in an effort to delay work, and she is later jailed because of her efforts. Mona, another character concerned about the environment, tosses a cigarette butt out of the car window and then guiltily stops the car to retrieve it, aware that they are not biodegradable.

Mark and Mona are interesting but unrealistic characters. Mona is a chain-smoking exgymnast who repeatedly refers to Mike as "beautiful thing." And Mark is a teenager who tends a garden, maintains a home, and seems unmoved by his father's abandonment. Other colorful yet whimsical characters are Mike's aunt Caroline whom everyone believes is a witch, reminiscent of the conjure woman in African American literature made popular in Charles Chesnutt's short stories. She intuitively knows that more than the obvious burdens Mike and the others. Watching Red disappear as they cheer him on to victory was difficult for the

teenagers, but knowing that his death was the result of a childish bet between friends was worse. It was simple: if Red swam out to the buoy,
he would be the new owner of the "sky blue '65 Mustang" (*Red*, 99).
Swimming to the buoy seemed easy, but as he started back to shore the
current engulfed him.

Johnson's sense of picture writing shines through in *Looking for Red*.
Careful word choice allows her to create images that make each poetic
scene visible. Richard Jackson recalls Johnson's gift: "She always saw
something very clear in her mind and was able to encourage the reader
to see the same thing." Critics have applauded Johnson's effort, noting
precision in blending past and present incidents, satisfactory treatment
of themes, and authentic portrayals of adolescence. Angeli Rasbury of
Black Issues Book Review concluded, "*Looking for Red* is a daring and
rich book about a teen's sense of immortality."[13]

The setting of *Looking for Red* differs from the other books. Johnson
says she decided to write a book set in Cape Cod after spending time
there. It is not certain whether Red will continue to appear on the coast,
but it is clear that Mike will continue to look for Red in the corners of
her mind though she is "[n]ot the same" (*Red*, 116). When the novel
concludes, Johnson brings the narrative full circle, reminding readers of
the carefree days when Mike rode on the back of Red's bike, a new
reader gobbling words while riding in the wind.

NOTES

1. Angela Johnson, *Looking for Red* (New York: Simon & Schuster Books
for Young Readers, 2002), 19 (hereafter cited as *Red*).

2. "Meet the Geniuses," *CBS News Report* (October 5, 2003). Retrieved
from http://www.cbsnews.com/stories/2003/10/05/national/main576576.shtml
on July 10, 2004. Keyword: Johnson, Angela.

3. Nancy Vasilakis, "Review of *Humming Whispers*," *Horn Book Magazine*
72, no. 1 (Jan.–Feb. 1996), 79.

4. Mary Helen Washington, ed., *Black-Eyed Susans/Midnight Birds: Stories
by and about Black Women*, (New York: Doubleday, 1990), 281.

5. Hazel Rochman, "Review of *Humming Whispers*," *Booklist* (February 15,
1995), 1,072.

6. Carolyn S. Brodie, "A Conversation with an Award-Winning Author,"
School Library Media Activities Monthly 17, no. 10 (June 2001), 44.

7. Brodie, "A Conversation with an Award-Winning Author," 44.

8. Patty Campbell, "Vetting the Verse Novel," *The Horn Book Magazine* 80, no. 5 (Sept.–Oct. 2004), 612.

9. Campbell, "Vetting the Verse Novel," 613.

10. Campbell, "Vetting the Verse Novel," 614.

11. Nina Lindsay, "Review of *Running Back to Ludie*," *School Library Journal* 47 (Dec. 2001), 164.

12. Diane Roback, ed.,"Review of *Running Back to Ludie*," *Publisher's Weekly* 248, no. 43 (Oct. 22, 2001), 77.

13. Angeli Rasbury, "Review of *Looking for Red*," *Black Issues Book Review* 4, no. 4 (July/August, 2002), 74. Academic Search Premier, 13 December 2004. Keyword: Johnson, Angela.

Chapter Seven

Discovering Tradition

The rich story-telling tradition in the African American culture—it is art, dance, and music all rolled into one. I am lucky to be a part of this proud tradition.[1]

"[The rituals] are about our ancestors and how we remember them in this life. They are the reason we are who we are," David, Emily's best friend, says, prompting her to look closely at those who came before her (*Toning*, 94). Similarly, the contemporary writer is often influenced by literary tradition. When asked if she felt her work was situated within the African American literary tradition, Johnson simply replies, "I hope so." In the past, some black women writers purposefully searched for literary ancestors, particularly foremothers, as many of them were familiar with writers such as Jean Toomer, Langston Hughes, Richard Wright, James Baldwin, and other male writers. In 1972, Alice Walker wrote her groundbreaking essay, "In Search of Our Mothers' Gardens," insisting that present-day black women writers owe their freedom to create to the existence of numbers of unknown African/black female artists. Walker argues that despite slavery, sharecropping, and abject poverty some black women still found ways to express their creativity. One of the most poignant aspects of the essay is Walker's claim that "often the truest answer to a question that really matters can be found very close. . . . The answer is so simple that many of us have spent years discovering it. We have constantly looked high, when we should have looked high—and low."

Like Walker, who found a link to black women's creativity in her mother's garden, Johnson's search seems to begin within her own family. She credits her father and grandfather for her love of story and storytelling and her mother for being supportive and believing that the writing she did while still an adolescent was exceptional. But when asked about favorite authors, she beams as she recalls the works of black women writers, particularly Virginia Hamilton and Maya Angelou. Both of these writers have claimed a significant place within African American literature, leaning on aspects of its literary tradition in their own work. Johnson also recalls that her teachers did not offer her books by African Americans. "I'd never heard of Zora Neale Hurston or Baldwin. . . . I wanted to read women."[2]

Within the book, also titled *In Search of Our Mothers' Gardens*, Alice Walker describes her search for literary foremothers, particularly Zora Neale Hurston.[3] Satisfied that black women writers contributed to the African American literary tradition, and American literature in general, Walker was free in her own creativity and in her ability to design and teach classes about black women writers. Since Walker, other critics have written extensively about black women writers. Henderson asserts, "One could . . . make the case that the founders of black American literature, in a formal sense, were women—Phillis Wheatley, Lucy Terry, and Harriet E. Wilson."[4] Black women writers occupy a unique position as American writers who create "within and independent of the American, Afro-American, and female literary traditions."[5] Several of the numerous characteristics of the black women's literary tradition involve putting black women and girls at the center of narratives as subjects rather than objects. Often black women's literature has sought to debunk traditional, stereotypical images of black women. Thus, black women writers create works that "represent black women in a variety of roles—as mothers, as daughters, as artists and writers, as wives, as domestic workers and teachers, as college students and world travelers, as beauticians, actresses: as subjects acting in history, as agents in their own lives."[6] Further, though this list is not exhaustive, works within the African American women's literary tradition often include an emphasis on one or more of the following themes and issues:

1. motherhood/mother-daughter relationships;
2. women-friends/women's work;

3. community;
4. sexuality; and
5. political activism.[7]

Many of these themes are found in Johnson's work and have been discussed throughout this book. *Toning the Sweep*, read and enjoyed by adults as well as young adults, and *Humming Whispers* are books that focus directly on black women's relationships with one another and how these relationships change over time. Other themes of significance in black women's literature, but scarcely seen in Johnson's work, are the interlocking oppression of race, class, and gender on black women and girls' lives and the pride of African American expressive culture.

INTERLOCKING OPPRESSION
OF RACE, CLASS, AND GENDER

African American women's literature is influenced by how black women perceive themselves and the world around them. Thus, identity is significant within African American women's literature. Though identity is socially constructed and constantly changing, race, class, gender, and sexuality are all components of one's identity and are critical in the formation of one's lived experiences.[8] The most basic efforts of black feminist theory, a useful theory for reading young adult literature, poses questions about the interlocking oppression of race, class, and gender issues on the lives of black women and on society in general.[9] For example, the way that black women were sexually violated during slavery offers a historical glimpse at how the oppression of race, class, and gender operates in the lives of black women. Hence, issues that affect women and young girls are at the root of most black feminist studies. Johnson's work often focuses on the coming-of-age of black girls, making a black feminist reading of her work possible. As discussed earlier, *Toning the Sweep* and *Heaven* offer glimpses of the methods used by Emily and Marley as they are thrust into the process of identity formation. However, Johnson does not tend to focus on oppression due to race or gender, and her female characters are rarely in need of finding their own voice. They are both audible and visible. Instead, Johnson focuses more on disenfranchisement due to class. Class

disparity often puts characters in her stories at odds with the larger so-
ciety. This is one of the major themes running throughout *Gone from
Home: Short Takes*, *Humming Whispers*, *Songs of Faith*, and *The Other
Side: Shorter Poems*.

In *Heaven*, the families seem to be working class, but the Maples differ. The Maples are middle class; they indulge in luxuries not available
to the other families. Beauty pageants, tennis matches, luxury cars, and
classical music are all symbols of the Maples's middle-class status. Several times throughout the novel, the Maples are referred to as perfect. It
is suggested that the Maples's adoption of middle-class values (read
white values) point to this superficial ideal of perfection. Ironically,
Shoogy Maple tries to distance herself from her family because of their
privileges. Unlike her siblings, she gets angry when her parents buy a
Cadillac because it symbolizes middle-class values and it further dis-
tances the family from other families in the community. Shoogy seems
eager to rebel against capitalism and middle-class values. Even when
she shares some of her family's interests—for instance, her appreciation
of classical music—she refuses to admit this to her family. When her
mother enters the house while she is playing classical music, she abandons it in exchange for rap music, suggested symbols of notions of
whiteness pitted against blackness. Race does not contribute to oppression or adverse living conditions, but class does. This is alluded to repeatedly in *Gone from Home: Short Takes*.

AFRICAN AMERICAN EXPRESSIVE CULTURE

Expressive culture refers to the way in which cultural groups, in this
case African Americans, express themselves in terms of language use,
physical appearance—including attire, hair style, and texture—and other
modes of expression (i.e., music, literature, etc.). Johnson depicts cultural expression as an individual choice. The protagonist of *Heaven*,
Marley, is named after Reggae legend Bob Marley, whom Johnson lis-
tened to constantly while writing *Toning the Sweep*. *Heaven* also includes a reference to novelist Zora Neale Hurston and to events such as
the church burnings in the South during the 1990s. Social movements
and other events that impact the African American community are also
briefly mentioned in *Toning the Sweep*: the Civil Rights Movement and

the L.A. riots. African royalty and the West African custom of toning are also seen in *Toning the Sweep*. African folk traditions and supernatural beliefs (i.e., conjure, voodoo, and root work) are mentioned in such novels as *Toning the Sweep*, *Gone from Home: Short Takes*, and *Looking for Red*.

What isn't seen in Johnson's work is the use of African American Vernacular English (AAVE) or any strong focus on the politics of skin color, beauty, or hair texture and style. These aspects of African American expressive culture have traditionally been staples in black women's literature. Language use within African American novels is often reflective of the African American oral tradition.[10] Significant elements of the African American oral tradition—storytelling, proverbs, signifying, and spitting game—are scarcely found in Johnson's work, though storytelling is important in *Toning the Sweep*. Through story, Emily discovers family traditions, history, and a better understanding of her mother. Emily also learns of her family's strength, pride, and privileges. Emily's use of the video camera allows her to capture and collect stories about her mother and grandmother told by members of Ola's community. While videotaping stories, Sally Hirt tells Emily that her mother was fourteen when she found her grandfather's murdered body lying by his car near the woods. This information further propels Emily on her journey to learn more about her grandfather and the tension between Ola and her mother.

A monolithic black language does not exist, as blacks choose to express themselves in various ways. According to Smitherman (2000), blacks are not confined to one mode of language use within one conversation. Blacks often use AAVE, Mainstream American English, nonstandard American English, and even some foreign languages such as Swahili, Spanish, and Yoruba, among others, while talking to other blacks.[11] Nevertheless, it is interesting that Johnson's work does not include a variety of language use. The majority of the characters in her novels, short stories, picture books, and poems primarily use mainstream American English combined with the deletion rule (e.g., 'cause = because), while other characters use mainstream American English entirely. Though mainstream American English usage often marks class distinctions, researchers have found that a large number of blacks, regardless of class or educational attainment, still use some form of AAVE.[12] Perhaps Johnson's characters do not because she rarely uses dialogue in her narratives. But it is likely that it is due to

Johnson's determination to resist stereotypical images of African Americans because she knows a number of African Americans do not use AAVE. Additionally, Johnson's characters are middle-class blacks, many of which are the offspring of college-educated parents, for whom AAVE may not be the dominant mode of expression.

Physical beauty is a significant part of expressive culture. Unfortunately, within the black community a large part of physical beauty rests upon one's skin color and tone and hair texture. Only subtle references to African American characters' skin color — Shoogy and Bobby's brown legs and Feather's "caramel skin" — are included in her work. Perhaps those characters Johnson does not identify as black are white. She has suggested that the majority of her protagonists are African American, but their friends may be of any racial background. Interestingly, Mary Helen Washington suggests that there is a consistent obsession among black women writers with physical beauty. Further, she argues that this obsession is an indication of how black women writers are "deeply affected by the discrimination against their skin and the texture of their hair."[13] One of the most disturbing literary examples of this is Pecola from Toni Morrison's *The Bluest Eye*. Longing for looks similar to Shirley Temple's seems to be the only thing in Pecola's pathetic world she has some control over. If the discrimination Washington refers to has existed in Johnson's life, it is not manifested in her work as an obsession. Her limited focus on hair is more of a celebration of natural tresses.

Emily, the protagonist of *Toning the Sweep*, likes to style and cut people's hair, but she wears her own short, though she considers allowing it to grow because she wants dreadlocks like Ola's. She admires the older women, like Martha and the aunts, who are "free spirits" with "liberated hair" that literally flies about their heads.[14] Martha "cuts her hair short, and some times it sticks straight up, but she doesn't care" (*Toning*, 18). When speaking of her dreadlocks, Ola tells Emily, "I love the way my hair feels. I do wonderful things with it. Hair should be kept at home — not loaned out to people who want to put strange objects and creams in it" (*Toning*, 44). Here, Johnson seems to be in conversation with Gwendolyn Brooks: "You have not bought Blondine. / You have not hailed the hot-comb recently."[15]

Historically, black women's natural hair texture has been depicted as undesirable, unattractive. This has led some black women to, as Ola

says, loan their hair out to stylists so that it can be completely trans-
formed with chemical straighteners. It is only then that the woman believes she is more attractive and that she looks socially acceptable.
Through Ola, Johnson seems to suggest an appreciation of African an-
cestry and to make a political statement resisting standard notions of
beauty. Ola helps Emily, and readers, see black hair differently. Johnson
makes little use of common pejorative terms for black hair such as *kinky*
or *nappy*, and when she does use *kinky*, she reclaims the word, making
kinky hair something to be desired. Emily says of her own hair, "I can't
get all of it between my fingers, but I love the way the kinky waves
feel" (*Toning*, 45). Johnson refers to black hair in ways that affirm
African American hairstyles and textures while simultaneously suggesting that these hairstyles and textures are acceptable marks of
beauty.

AFRICAN AMERICAN CHILDREN'S
AND YOUNG ADULT LITERATURE

African American children's and young adult literature have only recently been recognized as literature worthy of scholarship and criticism
within studies of African American literature written for an adult audience.[16] As a result, the genre has its own purpose, aims, history, recurring themes, and tradition though there is some overlap with African
American literature written for adults. African Americans began ap-
pearing in American literature during the seventeenth century.[17] Initially, American literature, including literature for young people, was
written for white audiences.[18] *Clarence and Corinne; or, God's Way*
(1890) by Mrs. A. E. Johnson, recognized as the first African American
children's book, was not written for African American children.[19] In the
beginning, the majority of the writers for children were white, and often African American characters were depicted in stereotypical and de-
meaning ways. Langston Hughes defines the images of African Americans in books for children published during this time as problematic.
"[T]he children's booklets on Negro themes, other than the folk tales,
have been of the pickaninny variety, poking fun . . . at the little young-
sters whose skins are not white, and holding up to laughter the symbol
of the watermelon and the chicken."[20]

One of the earliest efforts to retaliate against the degrading images of African Americans in books for young people was the publication of *The Brownies' Book*, a magazine for children, which emerged in January 1920.[21] Created by W. E. B. Du Bois (editor), Augustus Granville Gill (business manager), and Jessie Fauset (literary editor/managing editor), the mission of the magazine was described in the following way:

1. To make colored children realize that being "colored" is a normal, beautiful thing.
2. To make them familiar with the history and achievements of the Negro race.
3. To make them know that other colored children have grown into beautiful, useful, and famous persons.
4. To teach them a delicate code of honor and action in their relations with white children.
5. To turn their little hurts and resentments into emulation, ambition, and love of their homes and companions.
6. To point out the best amusements and joys and worthwhile things of life.
7. To inspire them to prepare for definite occupations and duties with a broad spirit of sacrifice.[22]

Some writers might argue that the goals of *The Brownies' Book* are obsolete today. There are more African American writers and illustrators creating realistic representations of blacks. In the introduction of Terry McMillan's *Breaking Ice*, an anthology of short stories and excerpts from novels written by contemporary authors, she describes one of the major goals of the book: to trace the metamorphoses inherent in African American literature from the 1970s to the 1990s.[23] Without question, the focus of the literature has changed in some ways and remained the same in others. McMillan asks, "[H]ow much sense would it make in the nineties if folks were still writing 'we hate whitey' stories or, say, slave narratives or why we should be proud of our heritage (we've known it for a long time now—our children know it, too)."[24] Some of Johnson's work conveys a similar sentiment, though a number of African American writers for youth still seem to adhere to the goals of *The Brownies' Book*. McMillan continues to explain that contemporary black writers write out of "a wide range of experiences that are indicative of the time we live now."[25] Speaking specifically of the writers in *Breaking Ice*, McMillan argues, "Our backgrounds as African-Americans are not all the same. Neither are our perceptions, values, and morals."[26] This is true of contemporary African American literature for young people too, yet there are some themes and issues that resurface across the literature.

During the early years, writers such as Langston Hughes, Arna Bontemps, Virginia Hamilton, and a number of others sought to provide literature with realistic and authentic depictions of African Americans so African American children could feel proud and affirmed. These writers have made firm commitments to infuse hope, pride, and knowledge of African American history in young people in an effort to educate them about themselves. At the time, this was significant because of the dearth of literature for young people fulfilling this significant need. The importance of this was so great that numerous studies have been devoted to the subject. Most notably are studies done by Nancy Larrick and Rudine Sims Bishop.

In 1965, Larrick surveyed 5,206 children's books that were published within a three-year period, 1962 to 1964.[27] The survey revealed that only 6.7 percent of the books contained African American characters within the story or in the illustrations. Those books that did depict African Americans perpetuated stereotypical images and reduced the African American experience to nothing more than a "servant or slave, a sharecropper, a migrant worker, or a menial."[28]

In 1982, Sims surveyed 150 contemporary realistic fiction books for children through eighth grade that featured African American characters. Sims was largely concerned with audience, perspective, and authenticity. Specifically, she posed questions about the intended audience of the books, the authors' perspective, as well as the author's knowledge of African American experiences and traditions.[29] As a result, Sims created three distinct categories for the books: social conscience, melting pot, and cultural conscious. The majority of the social conscience books dealt with racial strife, particularly black-white conflicts and desegregating schools and neighborhoods. Sims posits that these books were written for whites with hopes of teaching white children tolerance. However, she also notes that the books convey a message to African American children as well: "White children have problems too."[30]

The melting pot books, according to Sims, portray middle-class values as if they are normative. They are usually picture books that, in the words of Toni Morrison, "situate [people of color] throughout the pages and scenes . . . like some government quota."[31] Importantly, Sims suggests that the racial backgrounds of the characters do not impact the story in any way.

In the third group, culturally conscious books, the story is told from the perspective of an African American character. These books also portray language patterns, values, and traditions that are reflective of African American people. Sims maintains that the culturally conscious books were written for African American children. When reading Johnson's work in light of past studies on African American literature for young people, her work is quite difficult to categorize. Are Johnson's books culturally conscious, or are they simply melting-pot books? And should they be limited to such classification? Johnson told Dianne Johnson-Feelings, "You know, there are children out there who have never seen a black face in a book. . . . These books [her books] are not just for black children. Black children will have a better life if white children are reading these books too."[32]

Johnson's work is culturally conscious, presenting an evolving view of African American culture. African American literature for young people repeatedly emphasizes African American heritage as well as family history; family, including extended family, relationships; the importance of learning and obtaining an education; religion in the African American community; and supernatural and superstitious beliefs. In addition to the above, Sims maintains that culturally conscious literature emphasizes "pride in being black, a sense of community among blacks, a sense of continuity, and, above all, the will and strength and determination to cope and survive."[33] Like Johnson, Sims's image-makers who write African American literature for young people chose not to focus on racial strife and racial oppression. To date, *Toning the Sweep* and *The Other Side: Shorter Poems* are Johnson's closest and greatest efforts toward creating culturally conscious work. A strong sense of the African American community, tradition, and love of family are intricate parts of *Toning the Sweep* and *The Other Side: Shorter Poems*. It is in these books that African American culture has some significance. The main characters do not just happen to be African American; they must be in order for the premise of the stories to work. Other books such as *Songs of Faith* and

Heaven are also culturally conscious but focus on the everyday experiences of young people who are grappling with difficult problems.

Johnson's work is grounded in the African American tradition even as it extends the tradition and provides a glimpse of what the future holds for African American young adult literature. Her work is written skillfully and purposefully so that it is not exclusive but inclusive; thus, her work, like all good literature, is seen as not merely African American but universal.

FINAL THOUGHTS

> My books are universal stories. The children in them happen to be African American.[34]

Since the third grade Angela Johnson has had a desire to write books that evoke tears, laughter, applause, and thought. She has done that, many times within the pages of the very same novel. She began her career as a picture-book author but has since proven her versatility and skill as a writer of poetry, short stories, and novels for young adults. Surprisingly, Johnson has no formal training as a writer. She simply writes. To prepare herself for writing, she looks about and within, observing, striving to understand the mysteries of human nature. Johnson's themes, then, come from those who are closest to her, particularly her father, brothers, nieces, nephews, and godchildren.

Johnson says, "I write from my heart." In the pages of her books are the things she cares deeply about, those things she is deeply invested in: ecology, human and animal rights, health issues, and tolerance of differences. She pours her emotional attachment on to the page, into fully developed main characters, characters readers care about. Richard Jackson agrees that Johnson writes about what she knows. This is especially evident in her selection of settings. Each book is set in a place that has personal significance for her. Thus, the vivid images she creates are clear to the reader whether she takes us into the desert, the enclaves of Shorter, Alabama, or the streets of Cleveland, Ohio.

Her books are largely devoid of racial tension. As an adolescent, she was quite aware of racial disparity. "I understood that racially and culturally sometimes I was a bit separate," she says. But she believes the divide she felt growing up was "less about race and more about understanding." This sentiment is expressed in her work. Her books are about love, loss, fear, and determination. Her African American protagonists stem from experiences she knows intimately. They are characters who take vacations to other countries and have parents who are in white-collar professions, are artists, or own businesses. While discrimination still exists in such a world, her characters are not preoccupied with it. It does not serve as an obstacle for them, just as it hasn't for Johnson.

Johnson's books add another window into African American experience, emphasizing that the culture is not monolithic, that there are many black experiences. With Johnson, the reader discovers stories rarely told: the bond between three generations of women made even stronger by grief in *Toning the Sweep*, extended family relationships in *Heaven*, an African American teen father in *The First Part Last*, mental illness in African American communities in *Humming Whispers*, desertion in *Running Back to Ludie* and *Bird*, and accidental death in *Looking for Red*. The themes she chooses are universal, and the experiences her characters have transcend race, celebrating the familiar axiom, "We are more alike than we are different."

NOTES

1. Henrietta M. Smith, ed., *The Coretta Scott King Awards Book: From Vision to Realty* (Chicago: American Library Association, 1994).
2. Dianne Johnson-Feelings, "A Conversation with . . . Angela Johnson," *Quarterly Black Review of Books* 2, no. 3 (April 30, 1995). Retrieved from http://proquest.umi.com.proxy.lib.ohio-state.edu on 18 March 2005.
3. Walker, *In Search of Our Mothers' Gardens*.
4. Stephen Henderson, introduction to *Black Women Writers (1950–1980): A Critical Evaluation*, ed. Mari Evans (New York: Anchor Press,1984), xxiii.
5. Lorraine Bethel, "This Infinity of Conscious Pain: Zora Neale Hurston and the Black Female Literary Tradition," in *All the Women Are White, All the Blacks Are Men, But Some of Us Are Brave: Black Women's Studies*, eds. Gloria T. Hull, Patricia Bell Scott, and Barbara Smith (New York: The Feminist Press, 1982), 178.
6. Mary Helen Washington, *Black-Eyed Susans/Midnight Birds: Stories by and about Black Women* (New York: Doubleday, 1990), 5–6.

7. KaaVonia Hinton-Johnson, "Expanding the Power of Literature: African American Literary Theory and Young Adult Literature," (Ph.D. diss., the Ohio State University, 2003).

8. Kimberlie Crenshaw, "Mapping the Margins: Intersectionality, Identity Politics, and Violence against Women of Color," in *Critical Race Theory: The Key Writings That Formed the Movement*, eds. Kimberlie Crenshaw, Neil Gotanda, Garry Peller, and Kendall Thomas (New York: The New Press, 1995).

9. KaaVonia Hinton, "'Sturdy Black Bridges': Discussing Race, Class, and Gender," *English Journal* 94, 60–64.

10. KaaVonia Hinton, "Language Use and the Oral Tradition in AAYA (African American Young Adult) Literature," *Ohio Journal of English Language Arts* 45 no.1 (Fall 2004/Winter 2005), 21–28.

11. Hinton-Johnson, "Language Use and the Oral Tradition in AAYA (African American Young Adult) Literature," 25.

12. Geneva Smitherman, *Talking That Talk: Language, Culture and Education in African America* (New York: Routledge, 2000).

13. Washington, *Black-Eyed Susans/Midnight Birds: Stories by and about Black Women*, xiv–xv.

14. Alice Walker, "Oppressed Hair Puts a Ceiling on the Brain," *Ms.* (June 1988), 52–53.

15. Gwendolyn Brooks, *Primer for Blacks* (Chicago: Third World Press, 1980).

16. William Andrews, Francis Smith Foster, and Trudier Harris, eds, *The Oxford Companion to African American Literature* (New York: Oxford University Press, 1997).

17. Violet Harris, "African American Children's Literature: The First One Hundred Years," *Journal of Negro Education* 59 no. 4, 540.

18. Violet Harris, "African American Children's Literature: The First One Hundred Years," 540.

19. Violet Harris, "African American Children's Literature: The First One Hundred Years," 540.

20. Langston Hughes, "Books and the Negro Child," *Children's Library Yearbook* 4 (1932), 109.

21. Dianne Johnson, *The Best of the Brownies' Book* (New York: Oxford University Press, 1996).

22. Johnson, *The Best of the Brownies' Book*, 337–38.

23. Terry McMillan, *Breaking Ice: An Anthology of Contemporary African-American Fiction* (New York: Penguin, 1990).

24. McMillan, *Breaking Ice: An Anthology of Contemporary African-American Fiction*, xx.

25. McMillan, *Breaking Ice: An Anthology of Contemporary African-American Fiction*, xx.

26. McMillan, *Breaking Ice: An Anthology of Contemporary African-American Fiction*, xx.

27. Nancy Larrick, "The All-White World of Children's Books," in *The Black American in Books for Children: Readings in Racism*, eds. Donnarae MacCann and Gloria Woodard (Metuchen, N.J.: The Scarecrow Press, 1972), 160.

28. Larrick, "The All-White World of Children's Books," 160.

29. Rudine Sims Bishop, *Shadow and Substance: Afro-American Experience in Contemporary Children's Fiction* (Illinois: National Council of Teachers of English, 1982).

30. Sims, *Shadow and Substance: Afro-American Experience in Contemporary Children's Fiction*, 17.

31. Toni Morrison, *Playing in the Dark: Whiteness in the Literary Imagination* (New York: Vintage Books, 1992), 15.

32. Johnson-Feelings, "A Conversation with . . . Angela Johnson," 4.

33. Sims, *Shadow and Substance: Afro-American Experience in Contemporary Children's Fiction*, 96.

34. "Children's Author Donates Book Profits," 7A.

Selected Bibliography

PRIMARY SOURCES

Young Adult Novels

Bird. New York: Dial Books, 2004. (Paperback: Dial Books, 2004.)

The First Part Last. New York: Simon & Schuster Books for Young Readers, 2003. (Paperback: Simon & Schuster Children's Publishing, 2005; Random House Audio Publishing Group, 2004.)

Heaven. New York: Simon & Schuster Books for Young Readers, 1998. (Paperback: Simon & Schuster Children's Publishing, 2000.)

Humming Whispers. New York: Orchard, 1995. (Paperback: Orchard, 1996; new hardcover: Sagebrush Education Resources, 1996.)

Looking for Red. New York: Simon & Schuster Books for Young Readers, 2002. (Paperback: Simon & Schuster Children's Publishing, 2003.)

Running Back to Ludie. Pictures by Angelo. New York: Orchard, 2001. (Paperback: Scholastic, 2004.)

Songs of Faith. New York: Orchard, 1998. (Paperback: Random House Children's Books, 2001.)

Toning the Sweep. New York: Orchard, 1993. (Paperback: Scholastic, 1994; new hardcover: Sagebrush Education Resources, 2003.)

Poetry

The Other Side: Shorter Poems. New York: Orchard, 1998. (Paperback: Orchard, 2000.)

Short-Story Collections

Gone from Home: Short Takes. New York: DK Publishing, 1998. (Paperback: Random House Children's Books, 2000; new hardcover: Sagebrush Education Resources, 2000.)

Middle-Grade Novels

A Cool Moonlight. New York: Dial, 2003. (Paperback: Puffin Books, 2005.)

Maniac Monkeys on Magnolia Street. Illustrated by John Ward. New York: Knopf, 1998. (Paperback: Random House Children's Books, 2000; new hardcover Sagebrush Education Resources, 2000.)

When Mules Flew on Magnolia Street. Illustrated by John Ward. New York: Knopf, 2000. (Paperback: Random House Children's Books, 2002.)

Children's Picture Books

The Aunt in Our House. Illustrated by David Soman. New York: Orchard, 1996.

Daddy Calls Me Man. Illustrated by Rhonda Mitchell. New York: Orchard, 1997. (Paperback: Orchard, 2000; new hardcover: Sagebrush Education Resources, 2000.)

Do Like Kyla. Illustrated by James Ransome. New York: Orchard, 1990. (Paperback: Scholastic, 1993; new hardcover: Hardcourt School Publishers, 1997.)

Down the Winding Road. Illustrated by Shane Evans. New York: DK Publishing, 2000.

The Girl Who Wore Snakes. Illustrated by James Ransome. New York: Orchard, 1993.

I Dream of Trains. Illustrated by Loren Long. New York: Simon & Schuster Books for Young Readers, 2003.

Joshua by the Sea. Illustrated by Rhonda Mitchell. New York: Orchard, 1994.

Joshua's Night Whispers. Illustrated by Rhonda Mitchell. New York: Orchard, 1994.

Julius. Illustrated by Dav Pilkey. New York: Orchard, 1993.

Just Like Josh Gibson. New York: Simon & Schuster Books for Young Readers, 2003.

The Leaving Morning. Illustrated by David Soman. New York: Orchard, 1993. (Paperback: Orchard, 1996.)

Mama Bird, Baby Birds. Illustrated by Rhonda Mitchell. New York: Orchard, 1994.

One of Three. Illustrated by David Soman. New York: Orchard, 1992. (Paperback: Orchard, 1995.)

Rain Feet. Illustrated by Rhonda Mitchell. New York: Orchard, 1994.
The Rolling Store. Illustrated by Peter Catalanotto. New York: Orchard, 1997.
Shoes Like Miss Alice's. Illustrated by Ken Page. New York: Orchard, 1995.
(Paperback: Scholastic, 1995.)
A Sweet Smell of Roses. Illustrated by Eric Velasquez. New York: Simon &
Schuster Books for Young Readers, 2005.
Tell Me a Story, Mama. Illustrated by David Soman. New York: Orchard, 1989.
(Paperback: Scholastic, 1992; new hardcover: Scholastic Library Publishing,
1991.)
Those Building Men. Illustrated by Barry Moser. New York: Blue Sky Press, 2001.
Violet's Music. Illustrated by Laura Huliska-Beith. New York: Dial, 2004.
The Wedding. Illustrated by David Soman. New York: Orchard, 1999.
When I Am Old with You. Illustrated by David Soman. New York: Orchard,
1991. (Paperback: Orchard, 1993.)

Poems

"From Above," in *Heart to Heart: New Poems Inspired by Twentieth-Century
American Art.* Ed. Jan Greenberg. New York: Harry N. Abrams, 2001, 25.
"A Girl Like Me," in *On Her Way: Stories and Poems about Growing Up Girl.*
Ed. Sandy Asher. New York: Dutton Children's Books, 2004, 3–5.
"Her Daddy's Hands," in *In Daddy's Arms I Am Tall: African Americans Cele-
brating Fathers.* Illustrated by Javaka Steptoe. New York: Lee & Low Books,
1997, n.p.
"Tuesday (Chattanooga, TN)," in *In Praise of Our Fathers and Our Mothers:
A Black Family Treasury by Outstanding Authors and Artists.* Ed. Wade Hud-
son and Cheryl Willis Hudson. East Orange, N.J.: Just Us Books, 1997, 53.

Short Stories

"Atomic Blue Pieces," in *The Color of Absence: 12 Stories about Loss and
Hope.* Ed. James Howe. New York: Atheneum, 2001, 41–49.
"D'arcy." Unpublished. Given to author on August 6, 2004.
"Flying Away," in *But That's Another Story: Famous Authors Introduce Popu-
lar Genres.* Ed. Sandy Asher. New York: Walker and Company, 1996, 6–17.
"A Kind of Music," in *One Hot Second: Stories about Desire.* Ed. Cathy
Young. New York: Alfred A. Knopf, 2002, 204–17.
"Our Song," in *Memories of Sun: Stories of Africa and America.* Ed. Jane
Kurtz. New York: Amistad Greenwillow Books, 2004, 95–105.
"Through a Window," in *On the Fringe.* Ed. Donald R. Gallo. New York: Dial,
2001, 63–74.

"Tripping over the Lunch Lady," in *Tripping over the Lunch Lady: And Other School Stories*. Ed. Nancy E. Mercado. New York: Dial Books, 2004, 1–16.
"Watcher," in *Love & Sex: Ten Stories of Truth*. Ed. Michael Cart. New York: Simon & Schuster, 2001, 183–93.

Essays

Johnson, Angela. "Family Is What You Have," *Horn Book Magazine* 73, no. 2 (March/April, 1997), 179–80.

Speeches

Johnson, Angela. "The Michael L. Printz Award Speech," *Young Adult Library Services* 3, no. 1 (Fall 2004): 26–27.

SECONDARY SOURCES

Articles

Farber, Susan R. "Bonding through Books," *School Library Journal* 43, no. 4 (April 1997): 57.
Gregory, Lucille H. "Angela Johnson," in *Twentieth-Century Children's Writers*, 4th ed. Ed. L. S. Berger. Detroit: St. James Press, 1995, 493–94.
Hade, Daniel D., with Lisa Murphy. "Voice and Image: A Look at Recent Poetry," *Language Arts* 77, no. 4 (March 2000): 344–52.
Hinton, KaaVonia. "Affirming African American Boys," *Booklist* (January 2005): 59–63.
"Johnson, Angela." *Contemporary Authors: A Bibliographical Guide to Current Writers in Fiction, General Non-fiction, Poetry, Journalism, Drama, Motion Pictures, Television, and Other Fields, New Revision Series*, vol. 92. Ed. Scott Peacock. Boston: Gale Group, 2000, 210–15.

Book Reviews

Bird

Engberg, Gillian. "Review of *Bird*," *Booklist* 101, no. 1 (September 1, 2004): 108.
Hinton-Johnson, KaaVonia. "Review of *Bird*," *The Dragon Lode* 23, no.1 (Fall 2004): 17.

The First Part Last

Neal A. Lester, "Review of *The First Part Last*," *Journal of Adolescent and Adult Literacy* 47, no. 5 (February 2004): 429–31.

Roback, Diane, ed. "Review of *The First Part Last*," *Publisher's Weekly* 250, no. 24 (June 16, 2003): 73.

Gone from Home: Short Takes

Hoogland, Cornelia. "Review of *Gone from Home: Short Takes*," *Journal of Adolescent and Adult Literacy* 43, no. 5 (February 2000): 501–3.

Heaven

Rosser, Claire. "Review of *Heaven*," *Kliatt* (November, 1998): 6.

Humming Whispers

Rochman, Hazel. "Review of *Humming Whispers*," *Booklist* (February 15, 1995): 1,072.

Vasilakis, Nancy. "Review of *Humming Whispers*," *Horn Book Magazine* 72, no. 1 (Jan.–Feb. 1996): 79.

Just Like Josh Gibson

Engberg, Gillian. "Review of *Just Like Josh Gibson*," *Booklist* 100, no. 12 (February 15, 2004): 1,077.

Hinton, KaaVonia. "Review of *Just Like Josh Gibson*," *Lansing State Journal* (May 9, 2004): 8E.

Looking for Red

Rasbury, Angeli. "Review of *Looking for Red*," *Black Issues Book Review* 4, no. 4 (July/August, 2002): 74.

Rosser, Claire. "Review of *Looking for Red*," *Kliatt* 36, no. 3 (May 2002): 11.

The Other Side: Shorter Poems

Rosenberg, Helen. "Review of *The Other Side: Shorter Poems*," *Booklist* 95, no. 6 (November 15, 1998): 579.

Running Back to Ludie

Lindsay, Nina. "Review of *Running Back to Ludie*," *School Library Journal* 47 (Dec. 2001): 164.

Roback, Diane, ed.,"Review of *Running Back to Ludie*," *Publisher's Weekly* 248, no. 43 (October 22, 2001): 77.

Songs of Faith

Isaacs, Kathleen. "Review of *Songs of Faith*," *School Library Journal* 44, no. 3 (March 1998): 214.

Lempke, Susan Dove. "Review of *Songs of Faith*," *Booklist* 94, no. 12 (February 15, 1998): 1,008.

Roback, Diane, ed. "Review of *Songs of Faith*," *Publisher's Weekly* 245, no. 2 (January 12, 1998): 60.

A Sweet Smell of Roses

Parravano, Martha V. "Review of *A Sweet Smell of Roses*," *Horn Book Magazine* 81, no. 1 (January/February 2005): 79.

Rochman, Hazel. "Review of *A Sweet Smell of Roses*," *Booklist* 101, no. 11(February 2005): 978.

Toning the Sweep

Burns, Mary M. "Review of *Toning the Sweep*," *The Horn Book Magazine* (Sep.–Oct. 1993): 603.

Hearne, Betsy. "Review of *Toning the Sweep*," *Bulletin of the Center for Children's Books* 46, no. 10 (June, 1993): 318.

Dissertations

Crews, Hillary S. "A Narrative of the Daughter Mother Relationship in Selected Young Adult Novels." Ph.D. diss., Rutgers, the State University of New Jersey, New Brunswick, 1996.

Hinton-Johnson, KaaVonia. "Expanding the Power of Literature: African American Literary Theory and Young Adult Literature." Ph.D. diss., The Ohio State University, 2003.

Interviews

Brodie, Carolyn S. "Angela Johnson: A Conversation with an Award-Winning Author," *School Library Media Activities Monthly* 17, no. 10 (June 2001): 43–46.

Engberg, Gillian. "The Booklist Interview: Angela Johnson," *Booklist* 100, no. 12 (February 15, 2004): 1,074.

Hinton, KaaVonia. Telephone interview with Richard Jackson, Richard Jackson Imprints, Atheneum, 2 December 2004.

Hinton, KaaVonia. Interview with Angela Johnson. Kent, Ohio, and via telephone, 6 August 2004 and 26 May 2004.

Nelson, Todd R. "Angela Johnson: Teenage Graceland," *Hope Magazine* (January/February 2004.) Retrieved from http://www.hopemag.com/issues/2004/JanFeb/signGraceland.htm on 24 March 2004.

Index

About the Author

KaaVonia Hinton is assistant professor in the Department of Educational Curriculum and Instruction at Old Dominion University in Norfolk, Virginia. Her specialization is English education with an emphasis in multicultural literature, particularly African American literature.